D1162466

Women in Baptist Life

Women in Baptist Life

Leon McBeth

BROADMAN PRESS
Nashville, Tennessee

Dewey Decimal Classification: 286
Subject headings: BAPTIST//WOMEN

Library of Congress Catalog Card Number: 78-54245
Printed in the United States of America.

Foreword

I have lived all my life in the mainstream of Southern Baptists. As the daughter of one Southern Baptist minister and the wife of another, I have watched the unfolding of our denomination's contemporary story close at hand.

The topic of women's role in Baptist churches has long been of keen interest to me. Since my early adulthood, I have had a focused desire to discern accurately our Lord's intention for women's role in his world. Of course, as a Christian woman, I have had very personal reasons for wanting to know the mind of Christ concerning my own personhood and my "place."

In recent years, prodded by writing and speaking assignments, I have delved into a more thorough study of Scripture material than ever before and also read widely concerning women in Baptist history.

Certain questions continually surface: Should women take leadership roles in the church? Are they to do God's work alongside men or subordinate to them? Does the Bible teach the everlasting subordination of women to men? What roles have women had in Baptist history? Discussions of these questions have increased in intensity in the last few years. There has been a growing need in our denomination to have some respected Southern Baptist historian take a long, cool look at the scene and report his observations.

Fortunately, one of our most gifted scholars has responded to this need. Dr. Leon McBeth, a former pastor and for the last twenty years professor of church history at Southwestern Baptist Theological Seminary, is eminently qualified for such a project. He writes: "The way we are grows out of the way we were. What *is* takes shape out of what *was.* . . . We have been shaped by our history. This means if we are really to understand this issue before us we must take a look at the way we were."

With this statement as his basic premise, the author portrays for us what Baptist women have done in their churches and denomination from the earliest years of Baptist history to the present.

Dr. McBeth is quick to affirm an even more important premise: Southern Baptists' ultimate authority on every issue is not history or tradition, but the Word of God and the lordship of Christ. However, those who agree that the Bible is the authoritative Word of God for our faith and practice do not always agree about its interpretation. Therefore, Southern Baptists have had a history of wide diversity of opinion on "the woman question," as some call it. The debate does not question women's service in the everyday work of the church, for that level of involvement is encouraged and welcomed. The controversy arises at this point: Is it right for women to serve in leadership, policy-making roles?

As this primary question takes shape, the author stays quite naturally in the role of historian. He is a careful observer of detail and can document everything he reports. Yet he writes with the freedom of one who is neither proving a particular point nor vindicating a specific perspective. His approach is both simple and insightful: he presents the data, examines the combination of factors involved, and unflinchingly draws objective conclusions.

In *Baptist History and Heritage* (Jan., 1977), Dr. McBeth wrote, "To ignore the contribution of Southern Baptist women would be to read history with one eye shut." He is one who views the scene with both eyes open. To my knowledge, no one else has focused so clearly on the contributions of women to Southern Baptists as Dr. McBeth does in this book. Women comprise 55–60 percent of most Baptist congregations. To a surprising extent they have helped determine the shape of the programs and practices of our churches today.

Most Southern Baptists are aware of women's faithful dedication and dynamic involvement in the cause of missions. They are less familiar with women's impact on stewardship, Christian education, and other aspects of the total life of the church, even while meeting much resistance. Many a pastor has said, "We'd be dead without 'em." There is ample evidence to document this tribute.

It may be that many will be surprised to find that Baptists have had women in leadership roles from the earliest days: as deacons, deaconesses, and even occasionally as preachers. However, Dr. McBeth objectively emphasizes that this is not proof, in itself, that such practices should be followed today. For there is evidence, also, in other times and places, that women were not allowed to speak or even vote in church. This does not prove, likewise, that we should apply such patterns today. History should instruct us, but we must not allow it to determine our decisions.

Inevitably, any discussion of the role of women in the church turns to the most controversial question of all: should women be ordained and/or be allowed to serve as deacons and ministers today? The author does not sidestep the debate. Again he reports what has been and what is. He includes representative reactions, pro and con, that he has gleaned from denominational annuals and periodicals, past and present.

On the basis of my own study and the resulting deep impressions, I affirm the findings and conclusions of Dr. McBeth. He has a depth understanding of Southern Baptists and a keen appreciation of our heritage. I am especially grateful for his sensitive perception, clear perspective, and balanced tone.

Today churches increasingly are confronted with the matters being considered in this volume. The Southern Baptist Convention consistently has refused to take a position on women's role in the church and related questions. The historic stance has been that each church is autonomous and must work out the answers within its own body.

As individuals and churches search for insight, wisdom and divine guidance, this book can serve as a valuable resource. It offers a wealth of information without taking a "position." It lends itself effectively to being taught and studied in large groups or small.

It is my hope that pastors and other leaders will plan and promote the study of this work. In our desire to discover, declare, and practice the whole counsel of God, let us open our minds anew to a fresh infusion of the Holy Spirit's thinking. Let us probe more deeply than ever before into biblical material and historical data.

Perhaps many readers will discover in these pages that they have had misconceptions concerning portions of our Baptist heritage. I trust all readers will be enlightened and even inspired as they move through some of these less familiar corridors of our denomination's great history. My brothers and sisters in Christ, let us walk together with both eyes open.

MINETTE DRUMWRIGHT

Preface

In twenty years of teaching Baptist history at Southwestern Baptist Theological Seminary, I have become increasingly aware of the need for a history of the role of women in our denomination. My first preference would have been for someone else, perhaps a woman, to write this story. When no one else undertook the task, or seemed likely to do so in the near future, I decided to offer this work.

The story of Baptist women deserves to be told, yet it presents special difficulties. Throughout this study I have been plagued by a scarcity of historical records relating to women. Most history is written by men, about men. There is far more recorded HIS-story than HER-story. Our Baptist heroes are well-known, but our heroines are mostly forgotten. I hope this book will in some small way help remedy that imbalance.

It has not been my purpose to deal extensively with either the Bible teachings about women or the contemporary issues facing women. Rather I have sought to set out in context, the historical development of the changing role of Baptist women from the seventeenth century to the present.

We have several excellent books on women in Bible times or Bible teachings about women. One thinks first of *Woman in the World of Jesus* by Evelyn and Frank Stagg (Philadelphia: Westminster Press, 1978), and *All We're Meant to Be* by Letha Scanzoni and Nancy Hardesty (Waco, Texas: Word Books, 1974). The missionary work of Baptist women has also received attention in such writings as *History of Woman's Missionary Union* by Alma Hunt (Nashville: Convention Press, 1964), and the older work *In Royal Service: The Mission Work of Southern Baptist Women* by Fannie E. S. Heck (Richmond: Foreign Mission Board, 1913). Two quarterly journals have devoted entire issues to a study of Baptist women. They are "Women and the Church," *Review and Expositor* (Winter, 1975) and "The Role of Women in Southern Baptist History," *Baptist History and Heritage* (January, 1977).

The challenges and opportunities facing Southern Baptist women today have been discussed in a number of fine recent works, like *Woman Alone: Confident and Creative* by Sarah Frances Anders (Nashville: Broadman Press, 1976), and *Woman Aware and Choosing* by Betty J. Coble (Nashville: Broadman Press, 1975).

Some may take it amiss that I should write on this subject. Can any man have the insight and understanding to discern and develop the scattered strands of Baptist women's history? If my masculine eyes have missed some of the subtle implications of women's involvement in Baptist history, I beg tolerance, and plead honesty, at least in bringing the data to light.

Others may become impatient with me for another reason, that I have not in these pages assumed the role of impassioned advocate. It is not my purpose to argue what should have been the roles of women in Baptist history but simply to tell what those roles have been and now are. However, I am not so naive as to suppose that the arrangement of the facts does not reveal something of my personal judgments.

Parts of this book appeared earlier as an article in *Baptist History and Heritage,* quarterly journal of the Historical Commission of the Southern Baptist Convention. I thank the commission, and its executive director-treasurer, Lynn E. May, Jr., for permission to use parts of that article here.

I thank all the people who helped with this project and blame none of them for its shortcomings. I particularly thank two capable Baptist women: my secretary, Joyce Mahaffey, who typed the manuscript while managing regular office routine and correspondence, and Minette Drumwright, who provided some of the research, read the manuscript, made helpful suggestions, and above all provided encouragement when I might have abandoned the project.

To the one Baptist woman who is life to me, my wife, Ada, I dedicate these pages. Though not ordained, she has been to me through the years not only companion but also counselor, teacher, and minister.

For me this book has been a demanding task, written amid heavy teaching duties and committee responsibilities. Surely the reader will forgive me expressing relief that it is done. Looking out my office window at the bright winter sunshine, I think I would rather take a walk than write another chapter.

LEON MCBETH

Contents

ONE

Southern Baptist Women Today

A New Sense of Identity

She was about twenty-four, attractive, single, and a committed Southern Baptist. She had recently enrolled in Southwestern Seminary in the School of Theology. As she sat in my office that day, she seemed perfectly at ease. Her gaze was direct and her voice steady when she said, "I feel God has called me into the ministry. I am here at the seminary to prepare to be a minister."

As a pastor and now for twenty years a seminary professor, I have counseled countless ministerial volunteers. One learns to look for a sense of divine call, a sense of genuine commitment, and the presence of gifts for ministry. All of these seemed to be present. These qualities had at least been recognized enough that a Southern Baptist church had recommended this young woman for admission to the seminary to prepare for some form of the ministry.

This young woman is no isolated case. She is typical of hundreds of highly committed and motivated women in our colleges and seminaries who are seeking meaningful ways to serve Christ and his people. Our daughters as well as our sons love the Lord and want to find a place in his service.

The Southern Baptist woman today is gradually assuming a more vocal stance in church and society. Of course, not all Baptist women are seeking ordination as ministers or deacons. No doubt many are content in the traditional roles assigned to them by our society and our churches. But increasingly, Southern Baptist women are breaking out of stereotyped roles and taking places of leadership in the church, the community, and the larger society.

A New Day

In 1964 the Watts Street Baptist Church in Durham, North Carolina, ordained Miss Addie Davis to the gospel ministry. Since then perhaps as many as fifty Southern Baptist women have been ordained, and some are now serving as pastors. Hardly less controversial is the ordination of Southern Baptist women deacons, a practice which began long ago but mushroomed in the 1970's.

Since 1973, every meeting of the Southern Baptist Convention has debated the role of women, making this perhaps the most controversial issue facing Southern Baptists today.

Because these developments are recent, some assume this is a new question for Baptists. However, the record shows that Baptists have been debating the role of women in religion since the seventeenth century. Moreover, the actual roles of Baptist women have fluctuated greatly over the past centuries. Perhaps a review of our history at this point will enable Baptist men and women to understand better what is happening, and perhaps even what ought to happen.

This subject abounds with contrasts. In 1929, when a woman first addressed the Southern Baptist Convention, several men tried to prevent her from speaking; when they failed, some walked out. In 1978 a woman drew the largest crowd as she addressed the Pastors' Conference before the Convention.

In 1885 women were excluded from the Southern Baptist Convention; in 1963 a woman was elected vice-president of that body, and in 1978 women composed 42 percent of its messengers.

In 1901 a few women were allowed to sit in the back of the classroom at Southern Baptists' only seminary, but they could not raise questions or write exams, and they could not receive degrees. In 1977 our six seminaries had more than sixteen hundred women students, plus women trustees, and women faculty, including at least two ordained ministers.

The role of women in Southern Baptist life is a controversial issue. Some Southern Baptist state conventions have gone on record either for or against ordination of women, and others may take such a vote in the future. Though information here is incomplete, probably hundreds of local Baptist associations have discussed the role of women in religion, and many of them have taken a stand on the issue. At least one association, in Kentucky, has excluded a church for ordaining a woman.

A New Woman

Who is the Southern Baptist woman and what is she doing? That question has no easy answer because there are so many Southern Baptist women. Probably the majority of them are as loyal, faithful, committed to Christ as they have always been, but are willing for men to take the lead in church. However, a growing number of Southern Baptist women of all ages are no longer content to take a backseat in church.

You may not always find the Southern Baptist woman only in the church kitchen or teaching nursery-age children. She may not always confine her church activity to the Woman's Missionary Union or the social committee. Today's Southern Baptist woman may be in the seminary alongside the men studying theology, the Greek New Testament, and styles of proclamation. She may be on the board of trustees of the seminary or on its faculty. She may be an officer of the Southern Baptist Convention or a regular member of one of its boards or agencies. She may be employed outside the home and earn as much or more than her husband. She may be single, in any of the ways one becomes single, and accustomed to making her own decisions.

In her local church, the Southern Baptist woman may exercise more leadership than ever before. At times in our history women could not even vote in church conference. Today's woman doesn't just vote; she may make the motion or chair the committees which call for votes. She may be on the committee to seek a new pastor, and increasingly she may chair that committee. She may be an ordained deacon, and a few women have been elected to chair the deacon group in their churches. Today's Southern Baptist woman may, in fact, be the pastor of her local church.

These changes are far-reaching and fundamental. They represent significant readjustments in Southern Baptist thinking and practice on the part of men and women. One senses that these developments are not passing fads but represent long-range alterations in Southern Baptist life. Indeed, indications are that the trend toward more leadership roles for Southern Baptist women may accelerate in the future. One respected senior editor, C. R. Daley of Kentucky, in commenting on current trends in Southern Baptist life said, "Ordaining women as preachers and deacons is another trend among Southern Baptists. It is only a trickle now but looks more and more like the beginning of a stream." [1]

New Roles and Old Roles Recovered

There is no doubt that Southern Baptist women today are pioneering new roles in church and society. In response to contemporary needs and challenges they are developing new skills and carving out new positions. Without taking anything away from today's pioneering efforts, a historian might point out that some of the activity of Southern Baptist women today is not that new. It might surprise the churches and the women themselves to discover that in our history, Baptist women rather routinely served in some roles that seem so radically new today. At least some of the "new roles" for Southern Baptist women today are merely dusted off relics from generations past when Baptists were far less rigid about proper roles for men and women in Christ's service.

For example, from our earliest history Baptists had women deacons and deaconesses. In early America some Baptist churches had deaconesses and elderesses. The Separate Baptists of the South, who formed the spiritual and theological basis for the Southern Baptist Convention, had women preachers and routinely accepted women deacons and elderesses. Even after formation of the Southern Baptist Convention in 1845, churches in the South often had deaconesses.

After about 1890 most Southern Baptist churches ceased to have deaconesses, and the practice largely disappeared until its recovery in this generation. There are many reasons for this change, and these will be examined more fully in a later chapter. Many Southern Baptist women and men alike, growing up in this century, are unaware that women once exercised more church roles than they have in this century. Today's resurgence of women to places of leadership in Southern Baptist churches and in the SBC may look more radical to some than it really is.

Roots of Revolution

No observer doubts that there is a significant awakening among churchwomen in America, including Southern Baptists. The evidence is overwhelming. Many observers feel this movement will reach a flood tide and transform our churches.

What is less certain is why this is happening. Why are Southern Baptist women forsaking traditional roles of quiet background support for more visible and more active leadership roles? Why here? Why now?

Observers are not fully agreed on answers to these questions. Probably there are multiple causes, and no one explanation alone is adequate. The following may not constitute a full explanation, but they are at least contributing causes.

Abundance of prepared women.—One inescapable fact is that Southern Baptist women are *here,* and they are better prepared for Christian service than ever before. Thanks to the American educational system, our daughters are as well educated as our sons. They are sensitive to spiritual needs and are as highly motivated to Christian service as men are.

It is one thing to discuss theoretically the leadership roles of women in church when few women are prepared for roles and fewer still desire them. However, when churches have an abundance of women eager to serve and well prepared for effective service, the question ceases to be theoretical. One Southern Baptist statesman suggests that the presence of prepared women will in the long run do more to determine the church roles of Southern Baptist women than our theology or biblical views.

Response to spiritual need.—No one can doubt that our society is burdened with devastating spiritual needs. Lost multitudes need witnesses, disintegrating families cry out for caring counselors, lonely people in hospitals or other institutions need chaplains, and stale churches need vital ministries of teaching, nurturing, and proclamation. The needs are real, and they are pervasive.

Repeatedly our people have cried out to the Lord of the harvest to call in more laborers. In these latter days many thoughtful observers feel God is answering that prayer but in ways neither men nor women expected. Amid such crushing spiritual needs in our land, an increasing number of Southern Baptists are willing to accept every pair of willing hands turned to Christian service. They welcome every voice raised for Christ, whatever its pitch; they are grateful for every servant of Christ regardless of which half of humanity that servant represents.

Response to the women's movement in society.—One must remember that Southern Baptist women are Americans too. They read newspapers and magazines; they watch television; and they are acutely aware of what has been called the "Women's Liberation Movement." Millions of women are employed outside the home, and they know firsthand the progress and problems of American women. They also know what women are doing in other denominations in America.

It would be naive, indeed, to deny that Southern Baptist women have been influenced by the trends toward greater freedom and options for women in America. The increased role of Southern Baptist women in the nineteenth century (out of which came the Woman's Missionary Union), was influenced by the suffragette movement of that time. It is not strange, then, that Southern Baptist women today should be influenced by their sisters around them.

However, to say as one person did, "the clamor of Southern Baptist women today is nothing more than a few women libbers who have invaded the church," is grossly misleading. Certainly there is far more to this movement than this statement allows. One cannot escape the deep religious commitment on the part of Southern Baptist women today.

Response to other denominations.—In 1956 an outstanding Southern Baptist woman, a former college professor and then head of one of the departments of the Southern Baptist Sunday School Board, spoke in a seminary chapel service. In her opening remarks she said, "If I were a preacher, I would take a text and preach, but of course a woman can't preach. So I shall merely read a verse and make some comments upon it." Then she said in an aside, "Last week I attended a conference of Christian leaders. The woman who was my roommate was an ordained preacher in another denomination. I have often wondered why women can be preachers in some denominations, but not in ours."

Southern Baptist women are aware of what is going on in other denominations, whether they approve or disapprove. Though they may not be aware of details, in general they know that most denominations in America now ordain women as deacons and ministers on an equality with men. This cannot help but have some impact on Southern Baptist women and is doubtless one factor in their own efforts to exercise more leadership roles in church.

Reinterpretation of Scripture.—For generations, Baptists along with others, have quoted Paul's dictum that women must keep silent in church (1 Cor. 14:33-35) and similar passages to exclude women from any significant roles in religion. Southern Baptists have always accepted the absolute authority of the Bible as the Word of God and do so today. However, a growing number realize that it is not enough merely to *accept* the Bible; one must also *interpret* it honestly and accurately. One does no honor to the Bible when he proclaims his unquestioning acceptance of it and then misinterprets it.

For good or ill, many Southern Baptists, men and women alike, are taking a new look at the biblical teachings on this issue. With study of the historical background of passages, careful linguistic study of the Hebrew and Greek texts themselves, and a careful exposition of the basic content of Scripture teachings, many Southern Baptists are now convinced the Bible does not forbid women to be active in Christian service. We will return to this theme in a later chapter and seek to show how and why some Southern Baptists are in the process of reinterpreting Scriptures which previously were thought to sideline Christian women.

Expanded concepts of ministry.—Still another reason for the increased role of Southern Baptist women is our expanded concept of ministry. There was a time when in Southern Baptist life the "ministry" meant being a preacher or missionary. Those were the only roles or models available for a minister.

Models for ministry have vastly expanded. Our churches today have ministers of education, ministers of music, ministers to youth, ministers to the aged, ministers of administration and finance. Other ministers serve as counselors or chaplains in hospitals, industry, retirement homes, the military, or schools.

Most Southern Baptist women who are now engaged in the ministry are in nonpreaching and nonpastoral roles. Without the expansion in our concept of ministry, it is doubtful there would be as many Southern Baptist women in ministry.

One may not find any one of these six causes adequate to explain what is happening in Southern Baptist life, and all of them together doubtless fall short of a full explanation. Assuming that those who say they are called of God really are, there remains an element of divine mystery. Who can say why God calls some and not others?

One Southern Baptist statesman, in commenting on women ministers, recognized God's sovereignty by saying: "God does things at certain points in history, being answerable only unto himself as to why. . . . At any point in human history God does what God wants to do with his servants, men and women, and may utilize their talents and deploy them as he wishes to further the gospel." [2]

While it would be misrepresenting this man to say he was advocating ordination for women, his remarks show an openness to God's sovereignty. The same man wrote of the growing number of women in our SBC seminaries that "any lack of serious assessment of these delightful handmaidens of Almighty God will not meet the smile of God." [3]

Southern Baptists and the New Woman

Southern Baptists have not ignored, to say the least, the new woman in their midst. The "woman question," as some call it, has dominated the national and state conventions of Southern Baptists in recent years. Those who know Southern Baptists are not surprised that on this issue, as on all others, there is a wide diversity of opinion among our people.

Reactions to the more active role of women have ranged from welcomed approval to grudging acceptance, to rigid rejection. One can find this total range of reaction in all segments of Southern Baptist life, from grassroots lay people to the clergy and denominational leadership. One cannot say that lay people oppose the ordination of women, while clergy approve; or that young people approve, while older people disapprove; or that approval or disapproval centers in any one group, region, or theological complexion. The most that one can say is that some people approve, some disapprove, and some take the Gamaliel approach and are just waiting to see if this is of God.

Though the role of women has been a controversial issue before the Southern Baptist Convention in recent years, the Convention itself has taken no official stand. Some messengers have sought to get the Convention to go on record disapproving the ordination of women or reprimanding any Convention agency that employed or recommended an ordained woman. But the majority of messengers have recognized that in Baptist polity, ordination is a matter for the local church and not for the Convention to determine. The Convention has never sought to discipline or disfellowship any local Baptist church that ordained a woman as a deacon or minister, though some local associations have done so. Individuals may differ on this issue, and specific churches, associations, and state conventions may have an announced position, but as of now one cannot say that Southern Baptists as a whole have any official position for or against ordination of women.

If Southern Baptists wanted to arrive at an official position on ordination of women, it is doubtful they could do so. Southern Baptists accept no ultimate authority this side of the Bible and the lordship of Christ. But those who accept the Bible as the authoritative Word of God may yet disagree about its interpretation. Southern Baptists have no official creed or list of accepted doctrines and practices to which all must subscribe. The Southern Baptist Convention is a voluntary body made up of elected representatives (messengers) from churches that voluntarily cooperate in missions, evangelism, and Christian education. The Convention cannot speak officially for the churches; neither can the churches speak for the Convention.

In 1925 and again in 1963 the Convention voted to adopt a doctrinal statement of "Baptist Faith and Message." However, this is a confession of faith and not an official creed. It was designed as a statement of what a group of Baptists believe and practice at a given time in our history. In no way can it replace or supplement the authority of the Bible, nor was it so intended.

This means that any Southern Baptist individual or group has perfect freedom, under the lordship of Christ and their liberty to interpret Scripture, to favor or oppose the ordination of women as they feel the facts warrant. However, such individuals and groups have no freedom to impose their views and practices upon all Southern Baptists or to announce their preference as "the" Southern Baptist position. Ordainers and nonordainers can and should be in full fellowship among us.

As of 1977, several state conventions of Southern Baptists had taken an official stand against ordination of women. These states include Arkansas and Oklahoma, among others. The Georgia convention specifically voted down a resolution forbidding denomination employees to participate in the ordination of women, and the Washington, D.C., convention voted to endorse the concept of equality of men and women in the church.[4] While these represent majority votes of messengers in attendance, doubtless there are some Baptists who oppose women's ordination in those states which approve it and some who favor it in those states which voted disapproval.

Another reflection of the diversity of Southern Baptist opinion on this subject comes from a Home Mission Board survey in 1977. This survey, conducted by HMB research assistant Clay Price, shows that while most Southern Baptists oppose the ordination of women as pastors, a surprising 75 percent would approve ordination of women for ministry in religious education, youth ministries, and social ministries. One-third of the respondents had no objections to Southern Baptist women being ordained as deacons, and two-thirds agreed that Southern Baptist attitudes toward the role of women in religion will change significantly within the next twenty-five years.[5]

The Way We Were

This introductory chapter has been an attempt to sketch very rapidly what is happening right now in Southern Baptist life. In limited space I have attempted to portray us as we are.

However, the way we are grows out of the way we were. What *is* takes shape out of what *was*. Nowhere is this more true than in seeking to understand Southern Baptists, and especially the issue of the role of women. We have been shaped by our heritage. This means if we are really to understand the issue before us, we must take a look at the way we were.

That is where this book comes in. This is a *history* of the role of women in Southern Baptist life. One should not be put off by the term *history*. This will be more than a mere listing of names and dates which some people mistakenly identify as history.

These pages will try to tell honestly and accurately what Southern Baptist women have done through the years. It is a story worth telling and may even contain some surprises. The reader may discover either that women were more involved in leadership roles in the past than most realized or that they were less involved than hoped.

The fact that women previously served as Baptist deacons and occasionally as preachers is no proof, in itself, that women should so serve today. The fact that at other times Baptist women could not speak in church, much less vote, is not necessarily a pattern for what they ought to do today. History can be instructive, but for Baptists it is not authoritative in the sense the Bible is.

Notes

[1] "Current Trends Among Southern Baptists," *Western Recorder,* August 5, 1976, p. 3.

[2] Charles H. Ashcraft, "I must say it," *Arkansas Baptist,* December 4, 1975, p. 2.

[3] Ibid.

[4] "Convention Roundup," *The Baptist Standard,* November 23, 1977, p. 9.

[5] "Women Ordination Favored for Non-Pastoral Roles," *The Maryland Baptist,* November 17, 1977, p. 3.

TWO

Women and Early Baptists

When Women Preach and Cobblers Pray

Dorothy Hazzard kept a small grocery shop in Bristol, England, and she made it a point to stay open on Christmas day. A devoted Christian, she rejected the baptism of infants and other practices and ceremonies of the state church which the law required her to attend. Keeping shop on Christmas was one way to protest what she and other "dissenters" regarded as pagan practices which had crept into the church.

Other devout believers in Bristol also desired reformation, and soon a small group of dissenters gathered around Mrs. Hazzard. She was outspoken, courageous, and apparently a natural leader. Often the group met for Bible study and worship at her house. Hearing of "godly ministers," members of the group would sometimes go great distances to hear them, either in churches or in open fields or meadows. They would take notes on these sermons, and later repeat them for the group. Bristol was scandalized by this band, partly because they forsook the state church, but more because they allowed women to teach and preach. There can be no doubt that Dorothy Hazzard did both.

At Eastertime, 1640, John Canne, a Baptist preacher, came to Bristol. Mrs. Hazzard heard of his reputation for true religion, and went to hear him preach. Lydia-like, she insisted he stay at her house. Apparently she gathered the dissenter band, for an ancient record states "many of the professors . . . went thither to hear him, with Mrs. Hazzard." [1] When the authorities threatened Canne for preaching in Bristol, he preached out in the country seven miles from town. Wherever he preached, Dorothy Hazzard and her little band were there.

In Canne's Baptist faith the Bristol band found the truth they had been seeking. Dorothy Hazzard led them to accept believer's baptism and form themselves into the Broadmead Baptist Church. She was the first woman member and took a leading role in church life until her death thirty-four years later. Even the men recognized her courage, coming up with the best compliment they could in describing her as "like a he-goat before the flock." [2] As a teacher, preacher, Bible study leader, soul-winner, and founder of one of the most famous Baptist churches in England, Dorothy Hazzard left her mark.

Nor was Dorothy Hazzard alone in this work. To a degree which might surprise some today, women were active in leadership roles in early English Baptist churches. From the very beginning of English Baptist history, women served as deacons, deaconesses, hostesses to house-churches, and frequently as preachers. Baptist women were also active in America. Baptist women in the Middle Colonies served as deaconesses and elderesses, though this was less often true in New England. In the Southern Colonies the Separate Baptist women not only served as deaconesses and elderesses but also were known to "exercise in public." This latter phrase meant to preach, and among these original Southern Baptists numerous women were effective preachers.

This chapter will attempt to set out from historical evidence the role of women among early Baptists in England and America.

Women Among English Baptists

Baptists as we know them today originated in England in the early seventeenth century. As an organized denomination, Baptists emerged out of the left wing of the English Reformation. Two primary groups of English Baptists emerged in the early 1600s. Those called General Baptists had little use for predestination, believing that Christ died for all and that whoever would accept Christ could be saved. The General Baptist churches and denomination were tightly organized, with local churches giving up some autonomy to the denomination.

Those called Particular Baptists, on the other hand, were more Calvinistic in their acceptance of predestination. They believed that only the elect could be saved (thus their name "Particular"), and their churches were loosely organized to protect the autonomy of each church. Though both groups emerged at about the same time, women had a much more active leadership role among General Baptists than among the Particular Baptists.

Perhaps the earliest recorded comment on the role of Baptist women was by John Smyth, founder of the first identifiable Baptist church of modern history. In a 1609 work entitled *Paralleles, Censures, Observations,* Smyth wrote that "the Church hath powre to Elect, approve & ordeyne her owne Elders, also: to elect, approve, & ordeine her owne Deacons both men & woemen." [3]

The context shows that Smyth's emphasis was on the power of a local congregation to ordain elders (pastors) and deacons. Ordination did not require the authority of a bishop. However, he clearly acknowledged the place of women deacons as well as men deacons.

As early as 1607, before he led his church to adopt believer's baptism, Smyth had expressed similar views. In a work entitled *Principles and Inferences Concerning the Visible Church,* he described the officers of a church and their duties: "The Deacons are officers occupied about works of mercy respecting the body or outward man . . . . The Deacons are 1. men 2. weomen deacons or widowes. Act. 6,2. Rom. 16,1 . . . . Weomen deacons or widowes are of 60 yeeres of age, qualified according to the Apostles rule. 1 Tim. 5.9, releeving the bodily infirmities of the Saincts with cheerfulness." [4]

Smyth sets out a proclamation role for regular "prophets" of the church, apparently all men. He says that "All that have gifts may be admitted to prophesy 1 Cor. 14,31, Private persons are 1. men and 2. weomen."

In 1611, the same year the King James Bible came out, another early English Baptist leader, Thomas Helwys, issued a confession of faith. Article 20 of the Helwys confession states: "That the Officers off everie Church or congregation are either Elders, who by their office do especially feed the flock concerning their soules, ... or Deacons Men, and Women who by their office releave the necessities off the poore." [5]

This sets out the twofold ministry familiar to Baptists to this day, elders (pastors) and deacons (men and women) for ministry in material needs. The next article sets out how these officers were to be chosen, by "Election and approbacion off that Church," and how they were to be set aside "with Fasting, Prayer, and Laying on off hands." Evidently the women were ordained at the same time and in the same manner as the men.

From this and other evidence, it is clear that the earliest Baptists accepted women deacons. Apparently these women deacons were on an equality with men deacons, with the same election, ordination, and duties. However, the early English Baptist leaders apparently did not favor women preachers. The confessions that recognize women deacons are silent about women elders. In fact, Smyth bluntly stated that "Women are not permitted to speak in the church in tyme of prophecy." [6]

Despite such disapproval by some leaders, many women did preach, especially among the General Baptists. They were not formally ordained but neither were many of the men preachers. Baptists often faced ridicule, slander, and false accusations in England. Much of this centered around their form of ministry. Opponents charged Baptists with having a "mean ministry," made up of "base, mechanical fellows who cannot turn over Arabique." That is, Baptist ministers were ordinary working people, not educated in the universities.

This was mostly true, for Baptist preachers earned their livelihood as mechanics, tailors, soap-boilers, brewers, tinkers, and cobblers. Baptists did in that generation what herdsmen and vinedressers did in the early days of the Hebrew prophets, and what tax collectors and fishermen did in the early church. Perhaps it was a major strength of early Baptists that they were able to draw out and channel the natural gifts of ordinary lay people in preaching. Certainly the issue of women preaching is but one aspect of the recovery of lay preaching fostered by early Baptists.

Part of this opposition was that Baptists allowed women to preach, which seemed scandalous to upper-class Anglicans and Presbyterians of that day. The charge of allowing "she-preachers" sometimes took the form of rhyme, as the doggerel found in *Lucifer's Lackey, or, The Devil's New Creation,* part of which says: "When women preach and cobblers pray, the fiends in hell make holiday." [7]

The respected Presbyterian minister Thomas Edwards described Baptist growth in England as a form of spiritual gangrene (his work against Baptists is entitled *Gangraena, or a Catalogue and Discovery and Errors, Heresies, and Blasphemies*). One of his major accusations is that Baptists allow women to preach.

Of the Baptists Edwards says: "all sorts of mechanicks, taking upon them to preach and baptize as smiths, taylors, shoomakers, pedlars, weavers, etc., there are also some women preachers in our times, who keep constant lectures, preaching weekly to many men and women. In Lincolnshire . . . . there is a woman preacher who preaches (it's certain) and 'tis reported also she baptizeth, but that's not so certain. In the Isle of Ely (that land of eerors and sectaries) is a woman preacher also; in Hartfordshire also there are some woman preachers who take upon them to expound the scriptures in houses, and preach upon texts as on Rom. viii. 2. But in London there are women who for some time together have preached weekly on every Thursday, about four of the clock, unto whose preaching many have resorted." [8]

Edwards then describes at some length the preaching of these Baptist women, including a Mrs. Attaway, "the mistress of all the she-preachers in Coleman Street." From the emphases of Mrs. Attaway's sermon, we may surmise she was a General Baptist and a competent Bible student. Edwards complained also of "she-preachers in Kent, Norfolk, and the rest of the shires." Edwards was not alone in this complaint. The author of *The Schismatics Sifted* said: "Is it a miracle or wonder to see saucie boys, bold botching taylors, and other most audacious, illiterate mechanicks to run out of their shops into a pulpit? To see bold, impudent huswifes to take upon them to prate an hour or more?" [9]

Another complained of a woman who preached with such boldness and confidence that she "claps her Bible and thumbs the pulpit cushion" with great enthusiasm. Of her another said: "She with her Bible and concordance could preach nine times a week, morning and night."

From this and similar evidence, it is clear that Baptist women did preach in England in the early days of the denomination. It is equally clear that most English churchmen found the practice scandalous. Nevertheless Baptists opened the way for lay preaching and for women's preaching.

Where did the English Baptists get such ideas? For their views on the ministry, as on other questions, the Baptists went directly to the Bible for their authority. Those women who preached and

31

those men who allowed it thought they found adequate scriptural teaching and precedent.

Baptists were only one of many new groups which emerged in the seventeenth century seeking to recover New Testament faith and practice. Other groups in England included the Brownists, Independents, Separates, Quakers, and others. Most of these allowed women to be deacons and preachers. The Brownists took their name from Robert Browne who led a reform movement in the late 1580s. They had almost the same concept of ministry as the English Baptists who arose a generation later. The Quakers originated a few years after the Baptists and from the first had women preachers.

Baptists may have been more influenced by their religious environment than they realized. At that time to allow women to be deacons and preachers was a certain and vivid way to express rejection of the state church system, as well as to strike a blow for democracy and simplicity in preaching and worship.

Among Baptists, women deacons and deaconesses were far more common than women preachers. One early historian, Adam Taylor, says because of their strict attention to Scripture, the English Baptists "had only two orders of officers, Elders and Deacons; in which latter office they employed females as Deaconnesses." [10] Numerous examples of church minutes from dozens of churches amply verify this fact.

One is not surprised that the Bristol church, founded by Dorothy Hazzard, regularly ordained deaconesses although she was never one of them. The Bristol records show that on June 24, 1662, "sister West, a widow woman, was set apart to the office or work of a widow or deaconess in the church." [11]

The next year, because of the death of sister West, the church elected and by prayer set apart "sister Murray to be a widow or deaconness to the church." Many of the Baptist churches would have only one deacon and one deaconess, or at the most two. However, the Bristol church so grew that in 1679 they set apart "four sisters of the church that were widows, each of above sixty years of age, to be deaconesses for the congregation, to look after the sick sisters." [12]

At this time the church also outlined the duties of the deaconesses. They were to "visit the sick, to have their eye and ear open to hearken and inquire who is sick, and to visit the sick sisters." They were also to visit and minister to sick brothers, some thinking this was why they must be over sixty years of age to prevent scandal. They were to find out who was in need, visit and seek to meet those needs, and "make reports back of their condition" to the church. If they gave full time to this work and not only visited but also attended the sick, the deaconesses were to be "maintained by the church." This is one of the few indications that deaconesses may at time have been a salaried group among Baptists.

There was also a spiritual dimension to the deaconess ministry if we may take the Bristol church as typical. At the 1679 ordination of four deaconesses, the church said: "It is their duty also to speak a word to their souls, as occasion requires, for support or consolation, to build them up in a spiritual lively faith in Jesus Christ. For, as some observe, there is not an office of Christ in his church, but it is dipped in the blood of our Lord Jesus." [13]

From these records we gather that the office of deaconess was regarded as a scriptural office and that deaconesses were equated with the church "widows" mentioned in 1 Timothy 5:9. The deaconesses were set apart in the same manner as deacons, and they were expected to bear witness to their faith in personal work and evangelism.

The Bristol church was not alone in this practice. Church records are clear. If space allowed one might list numerous English Baptist churches with the names of their deaconesses and the dates elected. However, not all churches were as clear as Bristol about the deaconesses' duties.

In the earliest Baptist confessions, women were recognized as *deacons,* not *deaconesses.* For some people these were apparently convenient designations for men and women who performed the same task, much as one might differentiate between waiters and waitresses. However, very early a more distinct difference developed, and the deaconess was relegated to a nonordained role, distinctly inferior to deacons.

In other nonordained ways women were active in English Baptist churches. Converts who were "proposed for membership" were expected to give an account of their spiritual experiences. Women as well as men gave their testimonies before the congregation, often at great length. The records speak of congregations being "solemnly moved," "melted to tears," or "caused to rejoice in the Lord" after some woman's testimony of half an hour or more. In addition to Sunday worship services, many Baptist churches had Thursday fellowship meetings, often with a church supper. At these "social exercises" women as well as men asked questions, debated issues, and offered interpretations of Scripture.

Clearly, women were in the majority in most Baptist churches in England. One opponent ridiculed Baptists as composed of "Tradesmen & mostly women." In 1679 the Broadmead church had 166 members: 42 men, 108 women, and 16 (mostly women) excluded or under discipline. Perhaps their sheer numbers gave women added influence. From those churches that kept records of their contributions, it appears women were faithful contributors, but their total gifts seldom matched the total gifts of the men, however few.

When one English Baptist church sought a new pastor, it was a woman, a Mrs. Nethway, who made the long journey to Wales to hear a prospective pastor. Records show that "she being affected with his preaching, she was the instrument, when she came home, to persuade the leading brethren of the congregation that they were to endeavour to get the said Mr. Ewins to be teacher to this congregation, which, accordingly was assented unto." [14]

The usual custom among Baptist churches at that time was for a church to "raise up" a preacher from their own membership rather than call one from another church. However, when a preacher was called from another church, the calling church sought to get the church where the pastor then served to agree to release him. Sometimes they would, sometimes not. At times the women would simply prevent some popular pastor from leaving by massive prayer meetings, by sending delegations to the pastor to urge him to stay, and if all else failed, simply by refusing to vote to release him. In such cases, especially in early days, the pastor simply had to stay.

Women also took their lumps along with men during the persecution of Baptists. Women were fined, whipped, and jailed along with their menfolk. The earliest evidence of Baptists in Suffolk, for example, is the legal notice of September 30, 1644, that "bail was taken for the good behaviour of Thomazine Stott, who refused to go to church, confessing she was Anabaptist, and had lately been re-baptized, and had been ordered to gaol until she conform herself or adjure the realm." [15] At that time it was fairly common for Baptists to be called Anabaptists.

During times of persecution, women learned how to foil the authorities who burst in without warrants to search houses where Baptist worship was in session or suspected to be. Under the hated Conventical Act of 1664 such meetings in homes were against the law. However, this did not prevent Baptists from meeting; it just made them more careful. Due to a technicality in the law, the group could not be arrested if they were merely sitting in silence or singing a biblical psalm. Therefore, women who hosted these "house meetings" often led the group to an upstairs room and then had the women sit crowded into the stairway. They could hear and participate in the service, but if the authorities came unexpectedly the women could give the alarm and block the stairwell long enough to change the format of the service or even for the preacher to escape.

In one such crowded room, officers sought to arrest the preacher, but "sister Ekly, an ancient gentlewoman" barred their way by remaining seated in her chair. One officer picked up the chair, sister Ekly and all, but by then the preacher was safely out the window.

There were some truly remarkable women among early English Baptists. We have already taken notice of Dorothy Hazzard of the Bristol church. As a young widow she became the leader of a band of dissenters who would occasionally go out of their parish to hear preachers who had a reputation for godliness. In this way she met Mr. Hazzard, her second husband, who was a minister but apparently less zealous for reform than she. For some years Dorothy maintained a rented house just outside the parish boundaries. She would go to this house on Sundays, thus technically excusing herself from church attendance since she was out of the parish. During the week she used the house as a lying-in place for dissenter women so their babies could be born outside the parish and thus escape infant baptism.

It took courage to walk out on the minister, which Dorothy often did, but when the preacher was her own husband it was doubly delicate. Once when he returned from a trip and found her gone to hear a Baptist preacher, a neighbor "told him his wife was quite gone, and would hear him no more." Others deridingly said, "the next thing that followed would be that she would forsake the bed also." [16] However, Mr. Hazzard was apparently quite tolerant of his wife's religious convictions, and they lived together over thirty years, though there is no record that he ever became a Baptist. Dorothy was quite successful in personal evangelism, however, winning many to the Baptist way, including at least one state church minister. She died January 14, 1674, and was eulogized as "our aged sister Hazzard."

Katherine Peck of Abingdon also deserves to be better known. Apparently one of the founding members of the Abingdon church in Berkshire, Katherine and her husband, Simon, were frequently persecuted for their Baptist faith. Simon, a malster, was quite well-to-do and so his fines were heavy. Finally he agreed to return to the state church, but Katherine never did. After his death she continued the struggle to have a Baptist church; but for her courage and persistence, doubtless the church would have died. Known as one of the staunchest Baptists in the area, she was finally formally excommunicated. Later she was arrested, and in 1684 taken to London for trial. [17]

Ann Dutton was not a preacher or deaconess, but in many ways she was the most remarkable Baptist woman of her time. Born in 1692, she became a Baptist as a teenager and later distinguished herself as a writer. She left twenty-five volumes of letters to friends, and thirty-eight tracts and books on religious subjects. In her extensive autobiography, *A Brief Account of the Gracious Dealings of God with a Poor, Sinful, Unworthy Creature,* she appended a cogent defense of the right of a woman both to write and publish.

At age twenty-two Ann married a Mr. Cattle, but was soon widowed. When she transferred to the Cripplegate Church in London, before her husband's death, records show that "Ms Ann Cattle gave a Large and very choice account of the work of the Spirit of God on her soul to the great joy of the Church." [18] Evidently she was a good speaker as well as writer, and she ardently defended the right of women to do both.

In 1721, she married Benjamin Dutton, who was sometimes a Baptist preacher. Ann manipulated her poor husband (he was known as Mrs. Dutton's husband). When he was called to the Great Gransden church she agonized over the decision, regarding it as much a call to her as to him. She was sometimes egotistic, had a flair for the overly-dramatic, and evidently took some pride in her notable beauty. Despite these flaws, however, she was a capable and committed Baptist woman whose long years of faithful church service and extraordinary writing entitle her to a page in the book of memory.

From the evidence presented in this section, one may reach at least tentative conclusions. Clearly, Baptist women served in active roles in the churches, serving as deacons, deaconesses, and sometimes preachers. They were active in all church affairs, contributing money, voting on matters of concern, sharing in the calling and support of a pastor, speaking out regularly to give their Christian testimony, sharing in the discipline of the church, or simply sharing in worship and praise.

The role of Baptist women tended to diminish in England as the years passed. Women were quite active in the 1600's, still active in the 1700's, but less so by the 1800's. By the mid-1800's some churches had abolished the office of deaconess, and some even questioned the right of women to vote in church conference, much less to speak out. English Baptist women did not begin to reassert their historic leadership roles as deaconesses and preachers until the twentieth century.

Baptist Women in Early America

A woman's witness apparently led directly to formation of the first Baptist church in America. In early 1639, Roger Williams, a Puritan seeker (later to become famous for his stand on religious liberty), was persuaded by a remarkable Baptist woman, Catherine Scott, to make a public profession of his Baptist views. Governor Winthrop of Boston wrote in his journal, under date of March 16, 1639, that at Providence Master Williams being taken, or emboldened by Catherine, the wife of one Scott, to make an open profession of his Anabaptism, had formed a new church.[19] Williams was baptized and in turn baptized about a dozen others. He formed the church which has survived to this day as the First Baptist Church of Providence, Rhode Island. Probably the Scotts had become Baptists in England and were among Baptists known to have migrated to Providence Plantations before 1640. Catherine was a dynamic and capable woman (her husband was known as "one Scott, husband of Catherine"). Her sister, Anne Hutchinson of Boston, is probably the first woman preacher in America, but she was never a Baptist as some-times reported.

However, despite Catherine's influence, no great status can be claimed for Baptist women at that time. A few years later the Baptist church at nearby Newport listed the names of men members but did not even list women, children, or slaves, though all were included in the membership.

In Colonial New England, Baptist sentiments were expressed long before there were organized Baptist churches. Several people, includ-ing women, expressed their views by walking out of church during infant baptism or by closing their eyes and making a face during that part of the service. Governor Winthrop wrote of "The Lady Moody, a wise and anciently religious woman, being taken with the error of denying baptism to infants" who admonished by the Salem elders where she was a member, "but persisting still, and to avoid further trouble, she removed to the Dutch," (probably in New Amsterdam, later called New York).[20]

The role of women in church troubled Baptists in colonial America. In 1746, the Philadelphia Baptist Association debated the following query from one of the churches, "Query: Whether women may or ought to have their votes in the church?" The men delegates debated this issue for almost half a day, before concluding that women at least had a right "to give a mute voice, by standing or lifting up of the hands," to vote. They concluded that the silence of women in church could not be complete for then how could a woman give testimony to her conversion, how could she fulfill the Scripture to bring charges against an offending member in church discipline, or how could she defend herself if wrongfully accused.

For these weighty reasons, the brethren agreed that women had at least a limited right to speak in church. They said: "Therefore there must be times and ways in and by which women, as members of the body, may discharge their conscience and duty towards God and men . . . . And a woman may, at least, make a brother a mouth to ask leave to speak, if not ask it herself; and a time of hearing is to be allowed . . . yet ought not they to open the floodgate of speech." [21]

However, the association went on to say that the Scripture "ex-cludes all women whomsoever from all degrees of teaching, ruling, governing, dictating, and leading in the church of God," and while they may vote, if their votes are in any way unusual or fail to conform to the majority, they may be called upon to explain.

However, such restrictive views were not unanimous among Baptists in early America. Morgan Edwards, who in the 1760's served as pastor of First Baptist, Philadelphia, made several tours of the American colonies and reported on the progress and customs of Baptist churches. His book, *Customs of Primitive Churches* in 1774, shows that many of the Baptist churches had both deaconesses and elderesses; he also sought to defend the practice from the Bible. The work of elderesses he says: "consists in praying, and teaching in their separate assemblies . . . consulting with sisters about matters of the church which concern them, and representing their sense thereof to the elders; attending at the unction of sick sisters, and at the baptism of women, that all may be done orderly." [22]

Apparently some of the American churches made a distinction between elderesses ("elder women" of 1 Tim. 5:2) and deaconesses (Rom. 16:1) and widows (1 Tim. 5:9). Edwards went to great lengths to defend the biblical authority for elderesses and deaconesses, but there was no real difference in their work. Their election and ordination, he says, is much like that of deacons and elders. "The office of deaconess," he said, "is of divine original and perpetual continuance in the church. It is the same in general with the office of deacon." [23]

Despite this, Edwards sternly insisted that: "The Scripture forbids women to speak, ask questions, teach, dispute, rule, or vote in church. Yet they may make their minds known by means of a brother, and ought to have a just regard paid thereto." [24]

Women did vote in most Baptist churches in America, but Edwards regarded it as "a novel thing" unknown in earlier days. It also raised the practical possibility that "the women, who are always the most numerous, have in their power any time to decide everything against the men." [25] This provides the interesting insight that in America, as in England, women outnumbered men in Baptist churches.

One reason Baptist women in colonial New England and the Middle Colonies had less church role is that for the most part Baptists in these areas came from a Particular Baptist background.

As in England, the role of Baptist women in America tended to diminish after the end of the colonial period. David Benedict, a careful observer, said that around the turn of the century (1800): "The Baptists very generally in this country in former times decidedly approved females taking a part in social religious meetings . . . . Another portion of them, who are found chiefly in cities and populous places, are as decidedly opposed to anything of the kind . . . . This restraint on the freedom of the females, and the same may be said of the lay brotherhood, right or wrong, is evidently on the increase." [26]

The withering of women's roles in church and society came at about the same time, and probably for much the same reasons. Benedict's comment is interesting that as Baptist ministry became more orderly and authoritative, not only did women find less place but laymen did too.

The question of women voting in church continued to agitate Baptists, despite Edwards' effort to lay it to rest. In 1764, the First Baptist Church of Philadelphia refused to allow women to participate in the election of deacons. Edwards had been pastor here, and probably his influence is seen in this effort to withdraw suffrage from women. However, the women met in a separate assembly and framed a vigorous protest.

To the next business conference they brought a query "to know whether Women has a right of voting in that Church?" The brethren debated this issue but took no action. The sisters "soon let the Brethren know it was a Mistake." [27] The women complained that in the election they were passed over, as if they were "the most senseless of beings, the first instance that we ever knew of sisters being treated with such contempt in that church." Their basic point was that this church, from its founding in 1698, had allowed women to vote; this 1764 action in effect created a new ruling by disenfranchising the women. In defense of their action, the men referred to women's lack of suffrage in society as justification for its absence in the church.

At any rate, the Philadelphia church did not allow the women to vote in 1764 or for several years thereafter. During this time the church declined in spirit and attendance. Even so, women did have some role. When a young woman of this church who had trouble with her hip joint was alleged to have been cured by prayer and laying on of hands, the church appointed a committee of fifteen men and eight women to investigate her case. Both men and women signed the committee's report, but a note adds "The reason why we, the sisters, have signed this, is, because we have more narrowly searched her as to the hip." [28]

Other churches were more generous in allowing women to vote. "The Piscataway church took up the matter in 1819, when 'Brother Peter Runyon observed that he was "difficultied" in his mind because the Church debarred the sisters from voting in the church.' " At the next meeting it was decided "by a large majority that the sisters have an equal right, in all cases with the brethren, in voting, speaking and governing the church." [29] Two years later the Williamsburg Church of Penn's Neck took similar action, ruling "that a female member of the church have the privilege of voting on all church business." [30]

The First Baptist Church in Newark, as late as 1839, voted to "debar all female members from testifying at social meetings." This would include prayer meetings, as well as preaching services, and almost certainly meant they could not vote. When matters of church decision came up, the church would often call for "all male members" to meet for discussion and decision.

Baptist church discipline was stringent on the frontier, and women show up frequently in disciplinary action. The pattern was fairly standard, as numerous church minutes indicate. Often we read, "The church met, and after divine worship, proceeded to business." A reader almost gets the idea that worship was at times preliminary to the gossipy business sessions. It must have been fascinating to hear everything the members had done and said, even in private, reported in church in the most excruciating detail. Much of this discipline dealt with sexual offences, in which women had been "a Bused" by some man in the church. Interestingly, the church often dealt more harshly with the woman, even when the man was apparently the aggressor.

Quite often the problems between Baptist women were trivial, arising from frontier gossip, and hardly worthy of church attention. Certainly this was the case at the Cove Creek Church in North Carolina, which in February, 1818, dealt with the following: "A charge brought into the church by Sister N.V. against old Sister W. that she had a Bused her and called her a liar." [31] Almost every month the church was treated to a report of who had said what to whom, who had "given the lye" to somebody, who had "drunk to excess," who "stood for drinks," who gambled at horseracing, whose children had "attended a frolic," or who had been "a Bused."

By far the majority of these cases dealt with dissension among the women of the church, whether because they were more numerous or merely because they were more fussy. At any rate, despite their frequent triviality, they at least show that women were active members of Baptist churches, that they frequently spoke out in church to defend themselves or accuse others, and that offices or no they had a large influence on the life of the church.

Sometimes in church discipline cases, simply being a woman was an advantage. One woman, cited before her church for some offense, was released with the notation, "After considerable conversation on both sides, the church imputed some part of her misconduct to ignorance—she being a woman." [32]

Women Among the Separate Baptists

Having looked at the role of women in Baptist churches in England, New England, and the Middle Colonies, we now turn our attention to the Southern Colonies. Baptist women had their most active leadership roles in the South, especially among the Separate Baptists. Because of this, and because Separate Baptists were the original Southern Baptists, we must give more time to them.

Separate Baptists originated out of the sweeping revival known as the First Great Awakening. They were noted for fervent evangelistic preaching, emotional conversions, and uninhibited (and sometimes disorderly) styles of worship. Despite these problems, many saw in the revivals the true work of the Holy Spirit awakening dead churches and bringing the fire of true revival.

Separate Baptists sensed little acceptance in the staid New England communities, and the growing population of the Southern colonies offered more fertile fields. Leaders Shubel Stearns and Daniel Marshall with their families migrated to Virginia and on to North Carolina in the 1750's. At Sandy Creek, North Carolina (now Randolph County), they established the Sandy Creek Baptist Church in 1755. Within 17 years this church mushroomed from 16 to 606 members. It had sent out 125 preachers, who in turn had established 42 other

Separate Baptist churches and missions. Soon the Separate Baptists had spread like wildfire across North Carolina, South Carolina, Virginia, and into Georgia. Their main strength, however, was in the backcountry rather than the more settled coastal cities, where the more staid "Regular" Baptists had their greatest strength.

William L. Lumpkin, in his *Baptist Foundations in the South,* shows that Separate Baptists laid the groundwork for the present Southern Baptist Convention. The Separates set the tone in theology, evangelism, and organization which the Southern Baptist Convention later followed. However, in one area Southern Baptists have generally not followed the Separates, and that is in the role of women in church.

Whether from their General Baptist flavor, the needs of the frontier, or their study of the Bible, Separate Baptist women assumed a large church role. The Separate churches regularly ordained deaconesses and sometimes elderesses. In North Carolina an observer of Separate Baptist churches listed Sandy Creek, where "ruling elders, eldresses, and deaconnesses are allowed;" Shallow-Fords, where "ruling elders and deaconesses admitted," and Haw-River, where "ruling elders, eldresses, and deaconnesses are admitted." [33]

Most of the Separate Baptist churches also practiced the "nine Christian rites," including baptism, Lord's Supper, the love-feast, laying on of hands, washing feet, anointing the sick, the right hand of Christian fellowship, the kiss of charity, and devoting of children. Many of these, in addition to baptism and the Lord's Supper, survive in Southern Baptist life in abbreviated form. The Separates also had ruling elders as separate from pastors, and elderesses as separate from deaconesses. For a time they experimented with having "bishops," that is, pastors whose authority was acknowledged by all the churches in an area, but they soon dropped that idea.

The most notorious aspect of Separate life, however, was not the deaconesses but the popularity of women preachers among them. Without doubt, the leading example is Martha Stearns Marshall. As the sister of Shubel Stearns and the wife of Daniel Marshall, Martha was connected with the two greatest founders of the Separate Baptist movement. Described as "a lady of good sense, singular piety and surprising elocution, in countless instances [she] melted a whole concourse into tears by her prayers and exhortations." [34] Though

43

without formal training, as was also true of most of the men preachers, Martha Marshall preached extensively and effectively. It was her witness that won her husband to the Baptist faith, and she likely was involved in the fateful decision to migrate to the South. She set the pace for Separate Baptists, of whom Lumpkin says, "women prayed and spoke freely in public" among them.[35]

In several areas Baptist preaching was first introduced by women. For example, in 1783 there were but two Baptists, both women, in Westmoreland County, Virginia. One of the women invited Henry Toler to preach there, and he soon formed the Nomini Church.[36] Two women in Louisa County, Virginia, were converted by 1788 but had not been baptized because of opposition from their families. John Poindexter, the husband of one of them, was especially outspoken in his opposition to Baptists. However, his wife somehow persuaded him not only to allow Baptist preaching on his farm but also to donate land to build a church. Poindexter allowed his wife to be baptized, was later baptized himself, and became quite effective as a Baptist minister himself.

In addition to Martha Marshall, by all odds the leading woman preacher among Separate Baptists, one should also notice Margaret Meuse Clay and Hannah Lee. Margaret Clay of Virginia was recognized early as a woman of great ability. Though baptized by moonlight, she made no effort to hide her faith. She first made a name as a woman of prayer, being often called on to lead public prayer. Her home was a center for Baptist preachers, and she was fervent in faith. At one time she was among eleven Baptists arrested in Virginia for unliscensed preaching. She was carried to the courthouse for trial, where all eleven were found guilty and sentenced to a severe public whipping. Some unknown man paid the fine for Mrs. Clay, thus sparing her the beating. After the trial she went home singing: "Children of the heavenly king, as ye journey sweetly sing." [37]

Hannah Lee was a member of the planter aristocracy of old Virginia, well-read and with an inquiring mind. Her family was much offended when she became a Baptist. It must have been a trial to her family when in May, 1764, she was presented to the Grand Jury in Westmoreland on the charge of six months absence from the parish church. Widowed at an early age, Hannah later married Dr. Richard Lingan Hall, an educated man who joined her at Peckatone Plantation. Their marriage may have been performed by a Baptist preacher, but if so it would not have been legally recognized before 1780. In 1769 her older daughter married and inherited Peckatone Plantation, so Hannah and her husband moved to one of his plantations in a neighboring county. This new home rapidly became a center for Separate Baptist preachers, and Hannah was instrumental in getting several churches started in the area.

Hannah Lee Hall not only spoke out strongly for her Baptist convictions but also for the rights of women in church and society. Today she would be called a woman's libber.

This active role of women among the Separate Baptists did not fail to arouse oppostion from the Regular Baptists. When in 1755 Daniel Marshall sought ordination, a difficulty arose because Stearns was the only ordained preacher among Separate Baptists at that time. They believed it took at least two ministers to ordain. Stearns, therefore, sent for help to a neighboring Regular Baptist pastor, who curtly refused, declaring "that he believed them to be a disorderly set, suffering women to pray in public." [38]

Despite their difference, Baptists in the South toward the end of the colonial period felt a growing pressure to unite. The "Regular" Baptists centered in the cities and along the tidewater areas of Virginia, North Carolina, and South Carolina. Their theology was more Calvinistic. Though quite evangelistic, they preferred an educated ministry and orderly worship services. The "Separate" Baptists were scattered throughout the rural areas of the same colonies. Their theology was less Calvinistic, their evangelism more fervent, and their worship services often noisy and uninhibited. They also had more centralized ideas about denominational organization.

These differences created tensions and problems in efforts to unite the two groups of Baptists. However, probably the primary practical problem concerned the church role of women. The Separate Baptists, as we have seen, allowed women to be deaconesses, to speak out and testify in church, and even to preach. The Regulars allowed none of these privileges to women and looked askance at the Separates for doing so. Robert A. Baker in his *The Southern Baptist Convention and its People 1672-1972* cites as a major obstacle to the union of Baptists in the South, "the extensive ministry of women in the services" of Separates.[39]

However, the desire for unity eventually became greater than the problems, and by 1787 Baptists in the South merged under the name of United Baptists. The terms *Regular* and *Separate* were dropped, but the new name never really caught on. These United Baptists formed the basis of the Southern Baptist Convention which was formed in 1845. Thus the Southern Baptists of today are direct descendants of the Regular and Separate Baptists of the colonial South.

After the merger of Regulars and Separates, certain traits of each survived. The United Baptists (and later the Southern Baptists) largely accepted the Regulars' concept of ministry and doctrine. However, in warm spirit, fervent evangelism, and informal worship services, they more nearly resemble the Separates. The Separate Baptist tradition of the role of women did not survive in the new group. After about 1800, one reads no more about Baptist women preachers in the South, though more often of deaconesses. Women generally did not speak out or testify in church, and in some churches women were not allowed to vote. The Separate Baptist inheritance is basic to the present Southern Baptist Convention, and many Separate Baptist traits survive to the present. The Separate tradition of the leadership role of women, however, largely disappeared.

In this chapter we have looked at the role of women among English Baptists, Baptists in early America, and Baptists in the colonial South. In each area we have found that women were active speakers and leaders in Baptist churches, serving as deacons, deaconesses, and elderesses. In England and the colonial South, we have seen that women frequently served as Baptist preachers.

Therefore, the active leadership of women in Baptist churches is not new. Some of the emerging roles among Baptist women today are new; others reflect the reemergence of ancient Baptist practices.

There was no uniformity among early Baptists as to the role of women. Some churches had deaconesses; some did not. Some Baptists accepted women preachers; some did not. The records do not show any uniformity of duties for those churches that did accept women deacons and preachers. However, we gather that the office of deaconess was primarily a welfare office. The deaconess was to visit the sick, especially women where a visit from male ministers would at that time have seemed inappropriate. The deaconess was also to seek out those in need, and help distribute to them whatever assistance the church could afford, much as did the committee of seven in Acts.

Another duty of the deaconess was to assist at the baptism of women. In early days in England, Baptists were often accused of immodesty in the baptism of women, especially when such baptisms were at night. There are many accusations that Baptists even practiced nude baptisms, and they indeed may have at times. However, nude baptisms, if ever practiced by Baptists, certainly were rare, and one does not read of them at all after about 1675. Certainly the presence and assistance of a deaconess would be quite natural at the baptism of women, and doubtless this became a major duty of the Baptist deaconess.

The fact that Baptists once had deacons, deaconesses, and women preachers is no proof, in itself, that we ought to do so today. Certainly there are many other features of Baptist life in earlier centuries that are not found among Baptists today. In every generation Baptists have considered themselves under the lordship of Jesus Christ and the authority of the Bible and within those limits free to respond to needs as they see fit.

How does the role of Baptist women compare with women in other denominations? The next chapter seeks to answer this question by giving a brief sketch of the emerging role of women in selected American religious groups.

Notes

1 Edward Bean Underhill, ed. *The Records of a Church Meeting in Broadmead, Bristol, 1640-1687,* (London: J. Haddon, 1847), 19.

2 Ibid., 10.

3 William T. Whitley, ed. *The Works of John Smyth* (Cambridge: University Press, 1915), II, 509.

4 Ibid., I, 259.

5 William L. Lumpkin, *Baptist Confessions of Faith* (Valley Forge: Judson Press, 1959), 121-122.

6 Whitley, I, 256.

7 Quoted in Robert Barclay, *The Inner Life of the Religious Societies of the Commonwealth* (London: Hodder and Stoughton, 1876), 156.

8 Quoted in Rufus M. Jones, *Studies in Mystical Religion* (London: Macmillan and Company, 1909), 419.

9 Ibid., 421.

10 Adam Taylor, *The History of the English General Baptists* (London: 1818), I, 413.

11 Underhill, 72.   12 Ibid., 397.   13 Ibid., 398.

14 Ibid., 37.

15 Ashley J. Klaiber, *The Story of Suffolk Baptists* (London: Kingsgate Press, 1931), 18.

16 Underhill, 22.

17 S. F. Paul, *Further History of the Gospel Standard Baptists* (Gospel Standard Baptist Trust Ltd., 1969), VI, 289.

18 H. Wheeler Robinson, *The Life and Faith of the Baptists* (London: Kingsgate Press, 1946), 53.

19 James K. Hosmer, ed. *Winthrop's Journal: History of New England, 1630-1649* (New York: Charles Scribner's Sons, 1908), I. 297.

20 Isaac Backus, *Church History of New England From 1620 to 1804* (Philadelphia: American Baptist Publication Society, 1844), 51.

21 A. D. Gillette, ed. *Minutes of the Philadelphia Baptist Association, 1707-1807* (Philadelphia: American Baptist Publication Society, 1851), 53.

22 Morgan Edwards, *Customs of Primitive Churches* (no place or publisher noted: 1774), 41.

23 Ibid., 42.   24 Ibid., 102.   25 Ibid.

26 David Benedict, *A General History of the Baptist Denomination in America* (New York: Sheldon and Company Publishers, 1860), 940n.

27 William W. Keen, *The Bi-Centennial Celebration of the Founding of First Baptist Church of the City of Philadelphia 1698-1898* (Philadelphia: American Baptist Publication Society, 1899), 152.

28 Ibid., 154.

29 Norman H. Maring, *Baptists in New Jersey* (Valley Forge: The Judson Press, 1964), 94.

30 Ibid., 94.

31 George W. Paschal, *History of North Carolina Baptists* (Raleigh: The General Board of the North Carolina Baptist State Convention, 1955), II, 223n.

32 O. K. Armstrong and Marjorie M. Armstrong, *The Indomitable Baptists* (Garden City, New York: Doubleday and Company, Inc., 1967), 243.

33 Morgan Edwards, "Materials Towards a History of the Baptists in the Province of North Carolina," cited in *The North Carolina Historical Review* (July, 1930), 384-391.

34 Garnett H. Ryland, *The Baptists of Virginia 1699-1926* (Richmond: The Virginia Baptist Board of Missions and Education, 1955), 40.

35 William L. Lumpkin, *Baptist Foundations in the South* (Nashville: Broadman Press, 1961), 38.

36 William L. Lumpkin, "The Role of Women in 18th Century Virginia Baptist Life," *Baptist History and Heritage* (July, 1973), 163.

37 Ibid., 165.   38 Benedict, 684.

39 Robert A. Baker, *The Southern Baptist Convention and Its People 1672-1972* (Nashville: Broadman Press, 1974), 49.

THREE

Women in American Religion

Sisters in Other Denominations

The first woman preacher in America probably was Anne Hutchinson of Boston. In the 1630's she gathered the women of the community into her home weekly to discuss religion. She preached (though not ordained), taught, and debated religious questions. Sometimes she gave a public critique of Pastor John Cotton's sermon the previous Sunday, a practice that caused her no little trouble. Her meetings became so popular that some men began to attend. Described as a woman of "ready wit and bold . . . spirit," she was well-read and displayed considerable theological skill.

Anne Hutchinson offended the Puritan authorities because of her public preaching and especially because of her "antinomian" views. She was hailed before the Boston church in 1638 to be "reduced from her errors." However, the minister appointed to accomplish that task proved unable, for Anne Hutchinson held her own in the public debate, answering every argument. She rejected some of the righteous rigidity which marked American Puritanism at that time and advocated more spiritual freedom under the lordship of Christ.

Unable to convince her, the men excluded her from the church as an "American Jesabel," and delivered her soul up to Satan. As if that were not enough, they excluded her from the colony, thus forcing her and her family into exile. It was a tense moment as this convinced and capable woman turned to walk out of the church that had rejected her. As she proceeded up the aisle, suddenly a young woman arose and walked with her to the door. It was Mary Dyer. Twenty-two years later Mary would be hanged in Boston for being a Quaker preacher, the only woman known to be executed in America for religious reasons.

Mrs. Hutchinson migrated to Rhode Island, where she apparently continued her preaching, for we read that she "exercised publicly."

She must have been a woman of great courage thus to preach in a church where some doubted that women had souls. [1] This church was composed of a "mixed multitude," some of whom apparently had Baptist sentiments. Later a group led by Dr. John Clarke withdrew and by 1644 formed a Baptist church at Newport, the second Baptist church in America. This may explain why Mrs. Hutchinson is sometimes wrongly identified as a Baptist. Mrs. Hutchinson later migrated into New York state where she and her family were killed by hostile Indians.

Thus we see that America has had women preachers since our earliest colonial days. Today more than eighty denominations in America extend ordination and full church equality to women. The road from Anne Hutchinson to the women pastors of today in various denominations is long and winding. Though this book is primarily about Southern Baptist women, it might be instructive to compare their role with that of women in other denominations. This is by no means a complete history. Indeed, one might find entire books about women in any one of these groups. This chapter will attempt merely to cover the highlights of women in American religion.

Because the role of women in church closely parallels their role in society, it seems necessary to include the briefest summary of the "women's movement" in American history. For those interested in a fuller account of these movements, further reading is indicated in the bibliography.

Women in America

The current Women's Liberation Movement (WLM) is nothing new in America. The struggle for women's rights is ancient, and its American phase dates back at least to revolutionary times. The same hunger for freedom which triggered the American revolution led women to seek freedom and equality.

Colonial women were probably more active and equal than their sisters in England and Europe. The raw frontier, the shortage of women, and agricultural life meant that every pair of hands was valued. Colonial women could not vote or hold office but neither could most of the men at that time.

Men signed the Declaration of Independence, but women declared for independence too. Abigail Adams served notice to her husband who was helping draw up the American Constitution that: "I desire you would remember the ladies and be more generous and favorable to them than your ancestors . . . . If particular care and attention is not paid to the ladies, we are determined to foment a rebellion, and will not hold ourselves bound by any laws in which we have no voice or representation." [2]

Women did not receive equal rights at the birth of the nation, and though they did not "foment a rebellion" at once, the wheels of change were already in motion. The industrial revolution rearranged American life-style and propelled women into employment outside the home. Inventions such as the sewing machine gradually reduced the drudgery of home labor. Women were reading and aware and breathing the heady air of freedom.

Probably the abolition movement did the most to launch the nineteenth-century women's movement. Women delegates to the first World Anti-Slavery Convention in London in 1840, including a number from America, were relegated to the balcony and not allowed to speak. This pattern was repeated constantly in America. Women were among the originators of the antislavery movement, but found that before they could work effectively for that cause they first had to strike a blow for their own freedom. The women saw clearly the similarities in the subjugation of women and blacks in America.

Perhaps the London rebuff helped lead to the famous 1848 Seneca Falls Convention for women's rights. Elizabeth Cady Stanton was the prime mover, but other leaders included Lucy Stone, Anne Howard Shaw, Susan B. Anthony, and the Quaker preacher, Lucretia Mott. The Seneca Falls Convention issued a declaration of rights, purposely patterned after the Declaration of Independence, demanding that men have equal rights, nothing more, and that women have equal rights, nothing less. This movement was inclusive and far-ranging, demanding not only suffrage but also equal rights in property, family, divorce, employment, wages, and higher education.

After the Civil War the focus of the women's movement was narrowed primarily to the one issue of suffrage, perhaps with the hope that the vote would open the door to full participation in American society. Woman's suffrage was opposed by big business, the liquor industry, political bosses especially in the South, and both Roman Catholic and Protestant churches. All of these rightly perceived universal suffrage as a threat to their hitherto unchallenged domains. This early women's movement was intensely religious. Its leaders were church women, and its symbols and arguments grew directly out of Christianity. The women might have expected, and indeed did expect, the church to be their partner in liberation.

Even so, nineteenth-century women were acutely aware that the church was a large part of the problem. Their 1848 declaration looked toward the overthrow of the monopoly of the pulpit by males, and escape from "a perverted application of the Scriptures" which sanctions woman's inferior status. Despite these criticisms, early women liberationists were devout daughters of the church. It was the utter rejection by clergy and church that drove the movement out of the sanctuary into secular assembly halls. [3]

Then as now, some women felt uncomfortable with the more radical elements of the women's movement. As the movement became more thoroughly secularized by 1870, church women formed their own denominational groups. Most of these were formed for the ostensible purpose of foreign missions, but their original impetus represented a far broader spectrum of missionary, humanitarian, and leadership roles for women.

By the turn of the century, sentiment was building to grant women the vote. Some of the western states had already done so in order to facilitate the achievement of statehood, and eastern states looked longingly for some way to counteract the tide of immigrant votes. Perhaps the crucial factor, as far as churchmen were concerned, was the need for women's votes to win the prohibition crusade.

Women's suffrage was achieved by the seventeenth amendment, with Tennessee passing the final vote in 1920 on the strength of a ballot cast by a young Tennessee legislator at the request of his mother.

After 1920 the women's movement lapsed into dormancy, though it was soon clear that suffrage brought little change in women's status. Not until the 1960s did the movement experience a rebirth.

Most observers agree that the publication of *The Feminine Mystique* by Betty Friedan in 1963 awoke the long slumbering sisterhood and launched the current WLM. Today, as in the last century, the movement is not monolithic, but represents a wide spectrum of views and actions. While there is some sign that the church, both Catholic and Protestant, is more sympathetic to women's demands this century than last, the WLM is largely secular and indeed has sometimes targeted the church as a major oppressor of women.

There have been distinct advances in women's rights in recent years, such as Civil Rights Act of 1964, which outlaws sex discrimination in employment, improved opportunities for women in employment, education, athletics, credit, and health. However, as of early 1979 the proposed Equal Rights Amendment to the Constitution was still stymied short of adoption.

Women in American Religion

Most of the churches planted in colonial America came from a Reformation heritage. Of the major reformers, neither Martin Luther nor John Calvin saw many church leadership roles for women. Luther particularly took a chauvinistic attitude toward women, seeking to relegate them to their "place." Some historians think the reformers may have reacted adversely, consciously or not, to Catholic emphasis upon the Virgin Mary and the prevalence of Catholic nuns. However, churches of the Calvinist heritage accepted women into positions of church leadership far earlier than did churches of the Lutheran heritage.

During the colonial period only the Quakers had women preachers in any official sense. Many of the other churches had deaconesses, and in some cases women spoke out unofficially. Early in the nineteenth century, women took part in the revivals of the Great Awakening, many of them as exhorters and preachers. Most of the new religions which emerged in nineteenth-century America provided ministerial status and leadership for women, including Seventh Day Adventism, Shakers, and Spiritualists. However, the widespread ordination of women and acceptance of women as parish pastors is largely a twentieth-century development.

The Colonial Era

Most of the women preachers in Colonial America were Quakers. This group originated in England in the 1640's, emphasizing spiritual freedom in worship. Opponents named them "Quakers" from their habit of trembling or shaking during intense religious excitement. After their founder, John Fox, Mary Fisher was the first Quaker minister. However, this group did not ordain ministers, men or women, in any formal sense. Among them, whoever had a message from God was free to deliver it.

The first Quaker missionary to America was a woman, Anne Austin. Other Quaker preachers in those early times included Mary Allen Farnum, Mary Macy, Narcissa B. Coffin, and others. [4] One family, that of Joseph Hoag, provided almost a dozen preachers. All of Hoag's daughters became preachers, as did most of his sons and their wives.

Quakers helped establish Philadelphia, whose name means "brotherly love," but they experienced more hostility than love in early America. They were bitterly opposed not merely for their doctrines but perhaps equally for their acceptance of women preachers. They were often whipped, fined, and subjected to other indignities. In New England it was standard procedure for Quaker women preachers, when they were arrested, to be stripped naked and examined by Puritan authorities for any mark of Satan upon them.

In 1660 Mary Dyer was hanged in Boston; she was one of four Quaker martyrs in Colonial America. She was a woman of strong convictions and a well-known preacher among the Quakers. As early as 1638 she showed sympathy for Anne Hutchinson. Mary Dyer was described by Governor Winthrop as "a very proper and fair woman, . . . notoriously infected with Mrs. Hutchinson's errors, and very censorious and troublesome (she being of a very proud spirit, and much addicted to revelations)." [5] On a trip to England in 1652, she was converted to Quaker views and returned to this country in 1657 as a Quaker preacher.

Twice exiled from Boston and warned never to return, Mary Dyer persisted in preaching. In 1659 she was convicted, along with three Quaker men, and sentenced to hang. Two of the men were hanged at that time, but on the steps of the gallows Mrs. Dyer was pardoned on the condition that she would cease to preach. She refused, and the next year despite the pleas of many in authority, including Governor Winthrop, she was hanged. Observers remarked that "Mary Dyer did hang as a flag" to symbolize her faith.

The most famous Quaker preacher in early America was Lucretia Mott. She was born in 1793, and entered the ministry at the age of twenty-five. She also became an outstanding leader in various reform movements, including antislavery. She was one of the first women to grasp clearly that before women could strike a blow for the slaves, they would have to assert their own freedom as women.

Other than the Quakers and a few informal preachers like Anne Hutchinson, one finds little ministerial activity by women in Colonial America. Some of the New England churches had deaconesses, but few of them assumed speaking roles. However, the pastors' wives were an influential group in their own way. They kept the family together while their husbands were traveling, establishing churches. There are many such examples of wives who tended crops, cared for growing families, and kept the homefires burning in a most courageous way. Their names seldom appear in church records, but without them the pastors could not have done their home mission work. Perhaps many of the young ministers followed the advice of a veteran who advised them to "get wives of the old Puritan stamp, . . . those who can pail a cow, and churn the butter and be proud of a jean dress or a checked apron." [6]

Nineteenth Century

The nineteenth century was a time of change and reform in America. After the War of 1812, which confirmed the continued existence of the United States as a separate nation, efforts were made to change the way of life in this country. Among the reform crusades were antislavery, health reform, organized benevolence, and the women's movement. In each of these, women took a leading role. This helped prepare them, and the nation, for their increasing role in the church.

Women were prominent in the fervent revivals of the Second Great Awakening. This great nationwide revival, which broke out shortly after 1800, was marked by fervent camp meetings and new styles of evangelism. The camp meetings, beginning at Cane Ridge, Kentucky, changed many traditional practices. People gathered for miles around, cleared out a place in the woods, and held services at night by torchlight. The camp meetings were social as well as religious events and served to bring people together for late-summer campouts.

Thousands might attend one camp meeting. The preachers usually stood on platforms erected for that purpose, standing several feet above the ground. From these crude pulpit stands, the preachers would harangue the milling crowds. There might be as many as four or five preachers speaking at various places in the camp. People who wanted to be converted were invited to come to the front, to a clearing sometimes known as "the pen." These exhorters and praying people would work with them singly or in small groups.

The exhorter's function was to help the convert work through to conversion, to lead him to accept and act upon the preacher's message. A large number of exhorters were women, and they were known to be quite effective. This was a speaking role, at times almost a preaching role for women. Women were also prominent in the camp meeting singing.

Perhaps the greatest leader of the Second Great Awakening was Charles G. Finney, the converted lawyer credited with transforming styles of evangelism in America. Finney is often credited with taming the exuberant camp meeting and tailoring it to fit the local church, thus inventing the local church revival as it is known today. Finney's so-called "innovations" attracted attention. He allowed women to pray and testify in public. This gave a prominence to women in religion that was quite unusual for the 1830's.

Finney later served as president and professor of theology at Oberlin College and Lane Seminary in Ohio, schools with an early tradition for accepting women in ministry. Some historians also trace the Holiness-Pentecostal movement, which emerged from Methodism in the 1880's, to some of Finney's spiritual views. Perhaps in some limited way, therefore, the prominence of women preachers in the Holiness churches stems from principles of equality advocated by Finney.

The nineteenth century was a fertile era for the birth of new religious groups in America. The spacious frontier, religious liberty, and the religious excitement of the Second Awakening combined to create numerous new groups. Some of these, like Mormons, Disciples of Christ, and Seventh Day Adventism have survived to become major denominations today.

Many of these new groups were founded by women or allowed unusual leadership by women. The Shakers, America's first successful religious commune, was founded by Mother Ann Lee, who came from England to New York in the 1770's. Though married to a blacksmith named Stanley, Ann Lee preferred to keep her maiden name. She became convinced that she was the feminine incarnation of Christ, as Jesus of Nazareth was his masculine incarnation. She popularized the idea that God is both male and female.

The Shaker communities in America became famous for their immaculate farms, their practice of total celibacy, and their many inventions. What is today called early American furniture probably stems from their classic furniture. They are credited with such inventions as an improved straw broom, the wooden clothespin, the sulphur match, and the earliest form of the washing machine. Less well-known is their witness for absolute equality of men and women in society as well as in religion. Shaker women as well as men had perfect freedom to preach, teach, and testify, though there was no formal ordination among them.

The Seventh Day Adventist Church was founded by a sensitive young woman, Ellen Harmon White. From her youth, Ellen Harmon had been given to visions, revelations, and intense religious concern. Never robust, she was for a time caught up in the movement for reform of health and medical practices in America, an emphasis which has survived in the Adventist Church today. Later with her husband, James G. White, she was credited with the visions, insight, and determination which helped organize a church out of the millennial excitement of the mid-1880's. She was acknowledged as a prophetess in the movement, and women have always been accepted as preachers among Seventh Day Adventists.

Though not surviving today, the Oneida Community of the 1850's also allowed complete equality and freedom for women. This group was marked by their views of "complex marriage," by which every man was "married" to every woman in the community. This radical form of marriage often attracts so much attention that people overlook the other social implications of the Oneida Community, such as the effort to provide absolute equality of men and women in religion as in everyday life.

In 1848 two girls, Maggie and Katie Fox, perhaps inadvertently launched the movement which was to become the Spiritualist Church. From the first women were accepted as mediums, spiritual advisors, and speakers in that group. One notices that women are prominent in these roles in Spiritualism to this day.

Another new religion in the nineteenth century is Christian Science, established by Mary Baker Eddy. Not only was she a prominent teacher and preacher, but also women serve in these roles to this day in that church.

However, some of the new religions of that era definitely did not accept women ministers. Perhaps the most obvious example is the Mormon Church.

The first regularly ordained woman preacher in America was Antoinette Brown, who graduated from Oberlin in the class of 1847, and then studied theology for three years. She received one of the first theology degrees awarded to a woman. Though women had preached in America since the 1630's, hers was the first regular ordination. She was ordained on September 15, 1853.

As part of her education Miss Brown had studied sermon preparation and delivery and had been preaching since 1848. She later wrote nine books, and preached her last sermon at the age of 90. Reverend Luther Lee, in her ordination sermon, said: "We are not here to make a minister. It is not to confer on this our sister a right to preach the gospel. If she has not that right already, we have no power to communicate it to her . . . we are here . . . to subscribe our testimony to the fact, that, in our belief, our sister in Christ, Antoinette L. Brown, is one of the ministers of the new covenant, authorized, qualified, and called of God, to preach the gospel." [7]

At age thirty Miss Brown married Samuel C. Blackwell, and at that time "retired from pastoral labors." The mother of six children, she continued to write and preach, though she no longer served as a pastor. She was ordained in a Baptist church, though not under Baptist sponsorship.

After the Civil War the formal ordination of women as ministers became more common. Olympia Brown, who later married John H. Willis but insisted upon keeping her own name, was ordained in 1863 in Canton, New York. She attended the best schools of the day, with a master's degree from Antioch College and a theological degree from Canton Theological Seminary. Her first pastorate was in Massachusetts, where she labored with some distinction for six years. Then she moved to a much larger church in Connecticut, where she enjoyed another successful pastorate. The birth of a son in 1874 interrupted her pastorate only briefly.

Described as being "as well-furnished intellectually as any man ever was," Brown won a reputation as a skilled public speaker and disputant. This "champion disputant among women preachers," was a successful pastor, known as an outstanding preacher, published sermons, and preached before the national convention of her denomination. [8]

Two other women, Maria Cook and Lydia A. Jenkins, had preached acceptably for years among the Universalists in this area, but without formal ordination.

Ellen G. Gustin was ordained in Newton, Ohio, in 1873 by the Christian Church. Women had been preaching in that denomination, with considerable public acceptance, at least as early as 1860. Emi B. Frank was ordained in Indianapolis about the same time. Her ordination was approved without a dissenting voice, and "many of the ministers present gave public expression of approval of women in the ministry." [9]

Among the Universalists, Augusta J. Chapin was ordained in 1863 to labor mostly in the West. She helped establish the Universalist religion in San Francisco and later returned East, where she had a notably successful pastorate in Pittsburg. She is also known for a closely reasoned paper on "Woman in the Ministry." [10]

Phoebe A. Hanaford began preaching in 1867 among the Universalists, was ordained in 1868, and served pastorates in Connecticut, and the Church of the Good Shepherd in Jersey City. She conducted the marriage for her own daughter and often exchanged pulpits with her preacher son. She was the first regularly ordained woman in Massachusetts and the first regularly commissioned chaplain. A leader in her denomination, Hanaford regularly preached before the Connecticut state legislature and served on leading committees of her denomination. She once preached the ordination sermon for a male minister. [11]

Other ordained women of this group include Caroline I. James, Prudy Le Clerc, Eliza Tupper Wilkes, Lorenza Haynes (ordained at an advanced age), and Ada C. Bowles. All of these were regularly ordained ministers, and most served as pastors. Numerous other women preached regularly and served temporary pastoral assignments but without formal ordination.

As the Quakers furnish the best example of women preachers in the colonial era, the Unitarians and Universalists (later merged in

1961) led in the ordination of women after the Civil War. Ordained women are too numerous for even their names to be listed here. One might mention Clara Maria Babcock, the daughter of a Unitarian minister, who studied theology at Heidelberg, Germany, where she married the Reverend Herman Bisbee. After his death she was formally ordained and had a successful ministry as pastor. About the same time, Celia Burleigh was a well-known Unitarian pastor in Syracuse, New York.

One might also mention Sarah Perkins, a Universalist minister who gave birth to her second child the same week her new book was released by the publishers. Her husband brought the book to the nursery, laid it beside the little bundle of flannel, and exclaimed, "Rather smart woman to give the world a book and a baby during the same week!" [12]

These women pastors enjoyed the confidence and appreciation of their congregations. Fannie U. Roberts, a Congregationalist, preached faithfully to her church until bronchial tuberculosis destroyed her voice. Both her parents were pastors, and as a young woman she served for a time as superintendent of a Baptist Sunday School. As her voice weakened, she offered to resign her pastorate, but the church refused. Instead they raised money to send her out West to a different climate in an effort to recover her health. She died in 1875 at the age of forty-one. [13]

In addition to these women who were officially ordained as ministers, countless other women in many denominations were preaching in the nineteenth century. A number of these women became traveling evangelists, some with considerable following. Much like Aimee Semple McPherson and Kathryn Kuhlman in the twentieth century, these women were often excellent speakers, with a dynamic message, communicated with charm and personal attractiveness.

Maggie N. Van Cott achieved wide reputation as an evangelist among the Methodists. In 1875, at the age of forty, she conducted an unusually successful revival in the Clinton Street Methodist Church in Newark, New Jersey. [14] Described as "an exceedingly plain but scrupulously neat woman," she had wavy brown hair and a remarkably strong and impressive voice. People of all ages were converted in her meetings, mostly from the working classes. Some even compared her evangelistic success to that of Dwight L. Moody, who was active in city evangelism at the same time.

In one year, Mrs. Van Cott reportedly brought 1,735 people into the Methodist Church, traveled 7,208 miles in church work, and preached 399 sermons. However, the Methodist bishop refused her ordination because she was a woman. A number of other Methodist women were preaching at the same time, also without ordination.

Not a timid person, Mrs. Van Cott attended the famous Fulton Street prayer meeting one day in New York, which was attended almost exclusively by men. This was a noontime prayer meeting of influential businessmen, out of which, historians say, came the third Great Awakening. On the day she dropped in, Mrs. Van Cott took four or five minutes to pray and testify, feeling strongly the presence of God. At the conclusion, one of the men rebuked her for speaking in public, saying theirs was strictly a men's meeting and women should not speak out in public. She replied, "I thought I felt the Spirit of the Lord; and I am taught that, where the spirit of the Lord is, there is liberty." [15]

The range of work of these Methodist women is perhaps indicated by Amanda M. Way, described as "the friend of the slave, the champion of woman's rights, priestess of temperance." [16]

More colorful perhaps was Mrs. Lowrie, "a converted actress," who conducted a series of revivals in the Drew Methodist Church in Port Jervis, New York. Thousands attended, and over five hundred professed conversion. Observers said: "Mrs. Lowrie is an eloquent speaker, and an excellent vocalist. Her discourses are lively while she walks about the house. They are full of extravagant and impassioned passages, interspersed with weird hymns and wild gestures. She wields a powerful influence over the large congregation that assembles to hear her, and her voice is frequently drowned by their shouts." [17]

This is a revealing passage, particularly the emotionalism of Mrs. Lowrie's preaching. One recalls that within a few years many who preferred this style of worship and preaching withdrew from Methodism to form the early Holiness churches. In those churches, fervent, emotional preaching, and a tradition of woman preachers has continued.

Crises created by the Civil War cast women into new leadership roles in the churches, as in all of society. Even churches in which women preachers had been unknown found themselves more dependent upon women because of the shortage of available men. Even among Southern Baptists, women during these crisis years, often took the lead in church decisions and in securing pastors.

Another way in which nineteenth-century women distinguished themselves was in the growing Sunday School movement. Though Sunday School as we know it in this country probably originated as early as 1804 in Baltimore, it did not become universally popular until after the Civil War. From the first, women provided the vast majority of teachers in Sunday School, especially for Children, Youth, and other women. In most denominations there was resistance to the idea of a woman teaching a men's class or a mixed class of adults. This new role as Bible teacher gave women a new speaking-teaching role in the church, of vast influence. It also tended to show women, and others, that they could explain the Bible acceptably. Their role in Sunday School provided the experience, the vision, and the hunger for larger speaking roles in the church.

Probably Martin Marty is correct that the early Sunday School movement was "often opposed by ministers not simply because it was new or was a threat to established ways of doing things but because it was often in the hands of women." [18]

Almost all the major American denominations formed national missionary organizations for women after the Civil War. These national bodies grew out of local and regional missionary societies, which date from around 1800. Between 1868 and 1870, Congregational, Methodist, and Presbyterian women had formed national organizations for women to work in missions and related concerns. Within a few years, Lutherans, Disciples, and Northern Baptist women had followed suit. National organizations for women in all these churches sprang up almost overnight, but they express the growing role of women in American religion. They also represent the response of newly aware women capable, trained, and committed to the gospel and wanting a more vital role in American life, religious and secular alike.

Southern Baptist women were a few years later than most in completing their national organization. The Woman's Missionary Union (WMU), auxiliary to the Southern Baptist Convention, was formed in 1888, about twenty years after most denominations had formed similar groups. In her letters advocating a national organization of Southern Baptist women, Lottie Moon often pointed to the examples of other women, particularly Methodists, as a worthy example for Baptists to follow.

It would be a misreading of history to interpret these organizations exclusively in terms of missionary concern. It might be too strong to suggest, as some have done, that WMU was merely the Southern Baptist women's liberation movement of that time. But while foreign missions was the ostensible purpose, the organizations allowed women to meet, organize, control their own meetings, speak, debate, and persuade, as well as keep in touch with issues of the day. They also learned to raise and direct their own funds.

The post-Civil War years also saw a new wave of opposition to women's leadership in American religion. To deal with a few women preachers was one thing, but the arousing of millions of women in the missionary societies was something else. Almost every major denomination, including Southern Baptists, experienced a new wave of opposition from men to the idea of women speaking or leading in church. However the women may have viewed their mission societies, men often viewed them as churchly versions of the suffragette movement and opposed them accordingly.

In conclusion, one can see that the nineteenth-century women were moving steadily toward a greater role in the churches. This progress was encouraged by social conditions, the intense religious revivals, and the obvious success of those pioneer women preachers. New organizations, like Sunday Schools and missionary societies, also gave millions of women a new voice in religion and put them in a position to shape the church's ideas for the next century.

The Twentieth Century

American churchwomen probably lost ground early in the twentieth century. Continued opposition from men, hurtful identification with the secular women's movement, and a tendency to concentrate their energies on the suffrage struggle apparently gave a considerable setback to the role of women in the church. However, this movement broke out afresh in the 1950's, and in the past quarter century most major denominations in America have extended full ordination rights to women. To those developments we now turn our attention.

Presbyterian.—In 1956 the General Assembly of the Presbyterian Church in the United States added this simple sentence to its official description of ministry: "Both men and women may be called to this office." [19] With this simple sentence the Presbyterian Church became the first major denomination in modern times to grant full ordination rights to women. The first woman ordained by them was thirty-one-year-old Margaret Truman, a 1953 graduate of Union Theological Seminary. However, this represents a long struggle.

Ordination of women first came up among Presbyterians in 1872 when the General Assembly adopted rules to "forbid the licensing and ordaining of women to the gospel ministry, and the teaching and preaching of women in our pulpits." [20] Presbyterian women increasingly resisted this ruling. In 1912 Rachel G. Brooks, well-trained in theology, sought ordination but was rejected. In 1918 the Presbyterian church in Elmira, New York, engaged a spiritually mature woman in the church as supply preacher while the pastor was absent in France serving as a chaplain. The presbytery objected but later licensed the woman to preach in that presbytery alone. Higher church authorities forced the withdrawal of this license. A 1925 report on "Causes of Unrest Among Women of the Church" asked, "Does she [the Presbyterian woman] want to preach?" The report concluded somewhat ominously, "Not many do—as yet." [21]

Certainly Verdesi is correct in stating of Presbyterians that "many attempts to secure for women the privilege of ordination to the gospel ministry were made in the early decades of this century." [22] In 1930 and again in 1947 the church voted down proposals to ordain women as ministers, though they did agree in 1930 to ordain women as ruling elders, a lay office. Some synods ordained women in the 1920's, but the General Assembly refused to recognize them as valid ministers. In 1938 the church created a new classification called "CCW," or "commissioned church worker," for women. This recognized the professional woman church worker, but it was far short of ordination.

A 1953 report made clear that the Presbyterian church would ordain women, and in 1956 it was made official. However, by 1975 there were only 190 ordained women out of a total of over 13,000 ministers. [23] Even with ordination, Presbyterian women share the complaint of all ordained women; inability to get a church. Most of them serve as associate pastors, educational directors, or in some institutional capacity. Presbyterians also admit women as ruling elders and deacons, though the majority of these lay officers are men.

Methodist.—In 1956 the privilege of full ordination was extended to Methodist women, and today that church has more ordained clergywomen than any other major denomination in America. Though full ordination came late, Methodist women have long been active in the church. The Methodists produced the first woman faculty member in a theological seminary in 1837 and have produced a number of recognized women theologians. They had, as we have seen, their full share of women evangelists and preachers in the nineteenth century.

The Methodist church *licensed* women to preach in the 1920's, but this status meant they could not be presented to the Conference and thus could not receive a regular pastorate, though they could preach locally. After the ordination barriers were removed in 1956, the number of Methodist clergywomen rose from 246 in 1964, to 278 in 1968, and to over 500 today. The United Brethren Church, despite its name, had about 25 ordained women at the time of its merger with the Methodists in 1968. The first woman District Superintendent among Methodists was Margaret Henricksen in 1969. There are a number of husband-wife pastoral teams in the Methodist Church, and a few cases where husband and wife are pastors of neighboring churches.

Lutheran.—In the major Lutheran churches in this country, women have varying roles of leadership. Lutherans are generally more conservative on this issue than churches of a Calvinist heritage. In 1964 the Lutheran Church in America (LCA), one of the more liberal of the major Lutheran bodies, appointed a "Commission on the Comprehensive Study of the Doctrine of the Ministry." In its first report in 1966 this commission called for a greater role for women, and noted that concern over the "woman question" had been building since the mid-1950's, particularly in response to Presbyterians and Methodists. In 1968 this commission reported that no theological or biblical reasons barred women from ordination. It was no longer a moot question in 1968, for the denomination had twenty-four young women in seminaries preparing for ordination. In 1970 the LCA voted to extend full ordination privileges to women, and by 1975 had ordained twenty-four women. It also recognizes deaconesses, as do most of the Lutheran churches.

As with most denominations, women were actually functioning as preachers before the Lutheran church authorized their ordination. In addition to pressure from women within the LCA, this 1970 vote to ordain women may have been influenced by the example of Presbyterians and Methodists, plus the fact that for some years Lutherans in Europe have had ordained women.

Somewhat more conservative is the American Lutheran Church (ALC), where women up to recent times could not even vote in local church matters. A group of denominational leaders stated in 1968 that "there is no decisive theological argument against the ordination of women." Their position was that ordination for women is neither clearly forbidden nor demanded by Scripture, and thus they urged caution. However, by 1975 they had ordained five women.

Perhaps the most conservative of the Lutheran churches, especially on social issues, is the Lutheran Church-Missouri Synod (LC-MS). Only in 1969 did this church permit women to vote in local church matters, and not all churches allow even that. There is a restiveness among some LC-MS women, and this may have been a factor in the schisms which have plagued this church in recent years. One recent LC-MS statement says, "Those statements of Scripture which direct women to keep silent in church, and which prohibit them to teach and to exercise authority over men, we understand to mean that women ought not to hold the pastoral office." [24]

Disciples.—The Disciples of Christ movement is made up of several denominations ranging from the Christian Church to the more conservative churches of Christ. Some of these ordain women as ministers and some do not. As early as 1927 the Disciples had over 125 ordained women, and doubtless that figure is multiplied today.

Catholic.—Catholic women in America have shared generally the same lot as Protestant women in the church. Through their devotions and charity, Catholic women have been essential to the church but have had little leadership voice. In the ancient Roman Catholic Church deaconesses had a significant role. In the Middle Ages the deaconesses gradually declined, giving way to the new group of nuns. These Catholic nuns, often led by influential abbesses, Mother Superiors, and Reverend Mothers, exercised genuine influence up to modern times. However, in America several factors combined to reduce the role of nuns and increase their restiveness, especially in the twentieth century. They have been a mainstay of the Catholic parochial school system in America.

Women, including Catholic women, are not immune to their surroundings. Catholic women have been extremely sensitive to the fact that many Protestant churches are now ordaining women, and some Catholic women have claimed equal clerical status. The Catholic Church has officially strictly forbidden women to be ordained as priests. Barriers to ordination, according to Church sources, are the Pauline passages of Scripture, the Thomistic view of women as subject to man because of inherent biological inferiority to men, the commonly accepted identification of women with the Virgin Mary and thus with maternal and family roles, and the pressure of centuries of tradition. [25] Some Catholic theologians say the objection is basically cultural and traditional and that there is no valid theological reason to deny ordination to women.

Many observers thought Pope John XXIII may have opened the door a bit toward the ordination of women in his famous *Pacem in Terris.* He cited the right of all people to choose their way of life, including "the right to establish a family, with equal rights and duties for man and woman, and also the right to follow a vocation to the priesthood or the religious life." [26]

At Vatican Council II the Church officially gave women the right to proclaim the lessons and epistles at the mass, and in Catholic worship today one may often find women reading the Scripture lessons and some of the prayers. However, at this writing, the priesthood is still a man's world, because, say some church leaders, Christ and his apostles were all men. Roman Catholic women are making their views known, some through St. Joan's Alliance, an organization of Catholic women seeking a greater role in the Church. Some observers feel the 1976 ordination of women to priesthood in the Episcopal Church may lead to greater priestly roles for Catholic women.

In the Orthodox Catholic churches, women have even less role. The Orthodox churches represent Eastern Catholicism as the Roman Church represents Western Catholicism. Orthodoxy is often regarded as the most tradition-bound of modern churches. They have no women priests but do have an order of nuns. They do have deaconesses, and up to the twelfth century these deaconesses were ordained in a sort of "blessing." Orthodox women may study theology and serve as teachers of religion in schools. They may teach and even preach in lecture halls and schools but not in church. One spokesman summed up the position of the Orthodox Church by simply saying, "Women cannot receive the sacrament of ordination in the Orthodox Church." [27]

Jewish.—Like most others, the Jewish world has long been a man's world. But like others, that seems to be changing. From ancient times Jewish women have preached and prophesied but without formal prophetic credentials. Not until the past decade have American-Jewish women followed in the footsteps of their ancient kinswomen, Miriam and Deborah.

Judaism has been one of the most masculine-oriented religions. Women have occupied a secondary role in Jewish religion, as in Jewish society. The Jewish attitude toward women is reflected in a passage from the traditional prayer book in which men daily pray, "Blessed art Thou, O Lord our God, King of the universe, who has not made me a woman." [28]

The last decade has seen far-reaching changes. Sally Priesand was officially ordained as a Jewish rabbi in 1972 and later accepted a post as assistant rabbi at the Stephen Wise Free Synagogue in Manhattan. In her theological training she was usually the only woman in a group of men. Most of her fellow students accepted her, but some of her teachers refused to take seriously her ambition to be a rabbi. One even refused to sign her ordination papers. This first woman rabbi in America has had good success in her ministry. She is in the Reform branch of American Judaism.

The second woman rabbi in this country was Sandy Sasso, who at age sixteen decided to be a rabbi and persisted against all discouragements. After ordination she became rabbi at the Reconstructionist Havurah in Manhattan. Like Rabbi Priesand, she is affiliated with one of the more liberal branches of American Judaism. Rabbi Sasso's husband Dennis, is also a Jewish rabbi in a neighboring synagogue. They often discuss their work, share ideas, and work jointly to prepare sermons.

Episcopal.—Perhaps no major denomination has experienced a more bitter fight about the role of church women than has the Episcopal Church. This struggle and its outcome is important for itself, and also for its possible influence upon other denominations.

From early times the Episcopal Church (in England, called Anglican) has had devoted women, like sisters of charity. At different times in their history they have had orders of nuns and deaconesses, but until recent times the ordination of women as priests was out of the question. In 1882 an Episcopal observer said, "it would be deemed sacrilege by many in those churches for a woman to perform sacerdotal duties." [29] Sacrilege or no, many women are now performing such duties.

For years the efforts of Episcopal women for greater voice in the church fell on deaf ears. However, in the 1960's there rose a group of Episcopal women who refused to be silenced. Convinced of their call to ministry, convinced that the church needed them, and convinced they had something to offer, these modern women of varying degrees of militancy finally made their point.

One of their leaders was Carter Heywood, who grew up in the Episcopal church. Feeling a call to ministry, Ms. Heywood graduated from the prestigious Union Theological Seminary, only to find that every avenue to ministerial service was blocked. Under heavy pressure, in 1970 the church allowed women to be ordained as deacons on the same basis as men. In the Episcopal Church, unlike some churches where a deacon is purely a lay office, the Episcopal deacon has a semi-clerical status. Ms. Heywood was ordained a deacon in 1973 but found that this only renewed her desire to be a full-fledged priest. Against the advice of many, she and ten other women were illegally ordained in Philadelphia in July, 1974. Since many bishops sympathized with the women, it was not difficult to find three who would perform the ordination. This "bootleg" ordination attracted worldwide attention and was voted story of the year in 1974 by the Religious Newswriters Association.

Ranking leaders of the Episcopal Church denounced this irregular ordination as invalid and forbade the women to function as priests. However, the women continued to serve as priests, celebrating the Holy Eucharist, preaching, baptizing, and all other ministerial tasks. In 1976 the Episcopal Church voted by a narrow margin to allow ordination of women. A number of women have been ordained since that time, but harmony decidedly does not prevail. As in other denominations, the ordained women have difficulty being placed as pastors. Some bishops refuse to ordain women, refuse to allow women pastors in their dioceses, and threaten discipline against any church which accepts a woman priest. In England the Anglican Church has not ordained women, as of this writing, but appears on the verge of doing so.

Holiness and Pentecostal.—Without a doubt women have found more acceptance as ministers in the Holiness and Pentecostal churches than in mainline Protestantism. The Holiness movement emerged primarily out of Methodism in the 1880's and perhaps continued some of the emphases of early Methodism upon simplicity and sanctification. They also continued the tradition of women preachers, already well known in the more revivalistic wing of Methodism.

In the early 1900's the Pentecostal movement emerged out of the Holiness movement. Sometimes called "third blessing" people for their views that conversion, sanctification, and the charismatic gifts (primarily speaking in tongues) constitute three distinct works of grace, the Pentecostal churches have always had numerous women preachers. In fact, to this day most of the estimated seven thousand clergywomen in America are probably affiliated with some phase of the Holiness or Pentecostal movements. The beautiful and sensational Sister Aimee Semple McPherson, who established the Church of the Foursquare Gospel in the 1920's, is an example of the Pentecostal woman preacher. In more recent times Kathyrn Kuhlman became widely recognized as a television and crusade preacher-healer in what some call the Neo-Pentecostal movement. McPherson and Kuhlman have provided attractive and effective models for women who aspired to a ministerial standing in this century.

The New Religions.—Since about 1960 the United States has been flooded by a spate of "new religions," and some very old ones making their first stand in the West. Some of these include The Unification Church (Moonies), Hare Krishna, Children of God, Zen Buddhism, and others. Those with an Oriental background, especially those based in Hinduism, relegate women to a distinctly inferior role. The same is true of many new cults which have emerged out of Christian sources, such as the Children of God. However, in some of the truly new religions, women are admitted to full ministerial status on an equality with men.

In summary, we conclude that a woman in the pulpit is a common sight in American religion. Over eighty American denominations now ordain women, and this includes most of the major denominations, including Southern Baptists. Of the larger groups, those that do not ordain women include Catholic, both Roman and Orthodox; the Lutheran Church-Missouri Synod; and the Mormon Church. However, ordination does not always remove subordination. Women preachers still have trouble finding a pastorate. Most churches still prefer male pastors, and women pastors often have to accept the less attractive opportunities. Relatively few of them serve as pastors of large churches. Many serve as pastors of small churches, associate pastors, ministers of music or education, chaplains, counselors, or in other non-preaching roles.

Women in Other Baptist Groups

Southern Baptist women might be interested to compare their status to that of women in other Baptist groups. Baptists are a large and varied family, and they do not have unanimity on the proper role for women in the church.

Baptist women in England now serve as preachers and pastors. They baptize, administer communion, perform marriages and funerals, and generally do the full work of ministers. However, few of them are officially ordained for this role. In 1890 British Baptists created an Order of Deaconesses in London. However, this was a separate order of professional church women, more like Catholic nuns than the deaconesses who had served in English Baptist churches for centuries. The new Deaconesses were engaged mostly in social work. Their work, life-styles, and even their somber uniforms reminded one of the Salvation Army. British Baptists established living centers and schools for the Deaconesses, and gradually evolved a pattern by which they could go out to serve the churches as teachers, nurses, and social workers.

However, gradually the Deaconesses began to assume more distinctly ministerial roles. The absence of pastors during the wars, particularly World War II, demanded that deaconesses move into vacancies that could not be filled by men. There is an effort at the present to give equal training, ordination, and job assignments to both male and female ministers among the English Baptists.

European Baptists have a few ordained clergywomen, some of whom serve as pastors. European Baptists also have deaconesses and have had for generations. Baptists in Latin America have deaconesses, and several women have been known to preach but usually without official ordination.

In this country, the Freewill Baptists were the first Baptists to grant full ordination to women. This branch of the Baptist family also has the distinction of being an early advocate of racial equality, as evidenced by their ordination of black clergy long before most denominations. Freewill Baptist women formed the Freewill Baptist Female Missionary Society in 1847, and sent out Sarah P. Merrill and Lavinia Crawford, probably the first single women to serve as Baptist foreign missionaries.

The Northern Baptists (now called American Baptist Churches, or ABC) have a tradition of women preachers as early as the 1890's. American Baptists ordained Edith Hill Booker in 1894 in Kansas, Margaret M. Joshua in 1921 in Pennsylvania, and Gwendolyn Rich Thomas in Nebraska in 1940. They have long had women deacons, and in recent years they have a growing number of ordained women active in ministry.

The more conservative Baptists, such as General Association of Regular Baptists (GARB), Conservative Baptists of America (CBA), Baptist Missionary Association (BMA), and Primitive Baptists do not ordain women. Few of them allow women deacons. However, some of the fundamentalist Baptists have accepted the idea of women preachers. The ethnic Baptist groups (Swedish Baptists, Norwegian Baptists, etc.) usually do not ordain women as preachers, but they often do ordain women as deacons. At the present writing, most of the black Baptist groups do not ordain women, though some do.

This chapter has been an effort to set out the roles of women in various American denominations, past and present. Perhaps many readers would identify the primary role of church women with missions. The next chapter will sketch the role of Baptist women in missions.

Notes

[1] James K. Hosmer, ed. *Winthrop's Journal: History of New England, 1630-1649* (New York: Charles Scribner's Sons, 1908), Vol. I, 284, 297.

[2] Georgia Harkness, *Women in Church and Society* (Nashville: Abingdon Press, 1972), 87.

[3] Beverly Wildung Harrison, "The Early Feminists and the Clergy: A Case Study in the Dynamics of Secularization," *Review and Expositor* (Winter, 1975), 41f.

[4] Phoebe A. Hanaford, *Daughters of America* (Augusta, Maine: True and Company, 1882), 417.

[5] Jessamyn West, ed., *The Quaker Reader* (New York: Viking Press, 1962), 169.

[6] Roland H. Bainton, *Christian Unity and Religion in New England* (Boston: Beacon Press, 1964), 274.

[7] Hanaford, 423.   [8] Ibid., 426.

[9] Ibid., 468.   [10] Ibid., 426.

[11] Ibid., 428-9.   [12] Ibid., 436.

[13] Ibid., 457.   [14] Ibid., 463.

[15] Ibid., 466.   [16] Ibid., 455.

[17] Ibid., 455.

[18] Martin E. Marty, *The Pro and Con Book of Religious America* (Waco, Texas: Word Books, 1975), Con, 98.

[19] Elizabeth Howell Verdesi, *In But Still Out: Women in the Church* (Philadelphia: Westminster Press, 1973), 134.

[20] Ibid., 25.   [21] Ibid., 90

[22] Ibid., 133.   [23] Ibid., 18.

[24] Margaret Sittler Ermarth, *Adam's Fractured Rib* (Philadelphia: Fortress Press, 1970), 117.

[25] Ibid., 44.   [26] Ibid., 40.

[27] *Concerning Ordination of Women* (Geneva: World Council of Churches, 1964), 57.

[28] Cited in Priscilla and William Proctor, *Women in the Pulpit* (Garden City, New York: Doubleday, 1976), 134.

[29] Hanaford, 467.

FOUR

Baptist Women in Missions

Heathen Helpers Arise

Without Mary Webb, Lottie Moon might have finished out her days as a Georgia school teacher and never been heard of by Southern Baptists. No annual offerings are named for Mary Webb, and few even remember who she was. However, this tiny little woman, all her life confined to a wheelchair, probably did more than any other woman to arouse the Baptist denomination to missionary zeal in the early nineteenth century.

Born in Boston in 1779, Mary Webb ("Polly" to close friends) formed the Boston Female Society for Missionary Purposes in 1800. An observer might have dismissed this group of fourteen women led by a "hopeless cripple," as of little importance. However, they launched a movement and set in motion ideas which would eventually transform the Baptist denomination into one of the most missionary-minded groups of modern history. The Boston Female Society was perhaps the earliest women's missionary organization in America.

The impact of this little society and its dynamic founder was beyond calculation. It came into existence at a time when Baptists in America gave little thought to foreign missions. This society became the pattern for hundreds of similar women's mission societies which sprang up within a few years all over the new nation. By their Bible study these Baptist women began to recover the biblical message of missions, and doubtless shared these insights with their husbands, brothers, and pastors.

An early effort to involve Baptist churches in America in missionary work came with the well-known Massachusetts Baptist Missionary Society. It was formed in 1802 in the same church Mary Webb attended and was led by her beloved pastor Thomas C. Baldwin. Probably the missionary zeal and insights of the Baptist women in that church helped lead to the larger organization. Certainly the women were among its most faithful supporters through the years.

In the societies that sprang up among the Baptists, what did the women do? They met together, just as women. They learned to study the Bible, speak out and express their convictions, and pray as *women*. It was important to them that no men be present. In these societies Baptist women learned that they too had voices, and minds. They too could organize, promote, and lead. Their efforts to produce missionary leaflets and literature revealed that Baptist women could write. Though at that time few women earned or controlled much money, the women discovered that *regular* offerings of even a penny a week would eventually mount up.

The involvement of women is important for missions, but it went far beyond missions. The discovery of missions opened a door for Baptist women to more active involvement in the total church. The story of women in missions is vital to understanding the role of women in Baptist history. To that story we now turn our attention.

Early Missionary Societies

The earliest Baptist church in America was formed in 1639; the earliest foreign missionary was appointed in 1814. Why the long delay?

The churches in America, including the Baptists, had their hands full just surviving during the colonial era. The churches were few and scattered and had no effective ways to communicate and share information among themselves. Except for times of "awakenings," spiritual vitality was often at low ebb. The struggle for religious liberty exhausted much of the energies of Baptists. From earliest times Baptists in America sought to promote home missions among the Indians and on the frontier, but strange as it may sound to Baptists today, they gave little or no thought to foreign missions.

Almost overnight this picture changed, and Baptists developed an intense foreign mission commitment. Anglo-Saxon expansion in India made English-speaking people intensely aware of conditions in that land. English Baptists formed their Baptist Missionary Society in 1792 and appointed William Carey and others as missionaries to India. The ship schedules were such that English Baptist missionary appointees to India often traveled by way of America. Often they had long layovers, during which time these enthusiastic missionaries would reside in Baptist homes, where they shared their missionary zeal. Perhaps more important were the letters of William Carey to Baptists in America, urging the imperative of missions. Perhaps no one of these identifiable influences, and not all of them together, fully explains the missionary awakening among Baptists in the early nineteenth century. However, it seems clear that this awakening came among the Baptist women before it reached the men or the churches generally.

The Boston Female Society.—One historian describes the society formed by Mary Webb in 1800 in Boston as "the first woman's missionary society in the world." [1] Her story is worth telling again.

Crippled by an illness at the age of 5, Mary Webb never allowed her spirit to be bound. She was converted at an early age, but postponed baptism until she was 19 because she shrank from the ordeal of being wheeled down for a public testimony and the awkwardness of immersion in her condition. She had a keen mind and a bright friendly personality and apparently was immensely popular. At church young men competed in friendly rivalry for the privilege of lifting her tiny body into her regular pew. Her chair was then folded and parked at the end of the pew until needed again.

Miss Webb was deeply influenced by Thomas C. Baldwin, a Baptist minister who was her neighbor and friend before she joined his church. Baldwin was deeply influenced by William Carey's missionary movement, and perhaps his preaching helped influence Miss Webb. Baldwin encouraged her to be active, to resist becoming a recluse. Apparently the idea of forming a women's society in 1800 was entirely her own. Of the original fourteen members, eight were Baptist and six Congregational. For several years they divided their meager income equally between mission causes of the two denominations, but in 1829 came to a cordial separation so that each group could concentrate on its own denomination. At the time of founding, Miss Webb was only 21 and most of the other members were also quite young.

Miss Webb served as secretary-treasurer of the society for more than fifty years. In this capacity she wrote letters and reports, prepared financial statements, and conducted the business conferences of the group. Some of her letters were to "females professing godliness" in other denominations, and in 1812 they heard from 17 other such societies in different denominations. This correspondence shows beyond a doubt that the Boston group was a catalyst for similar groups elsewhere.

In addition to "missions" in the strict sense, Miss Webb led the Society to do many kinds of social and educational work. Several societies were spin-offs from the parent group, such as the Female Cent Society in 1803; the Children's Cent Society, first recorded as a society in 1811; the Corban Society, 1811, to raise money to help educate young ministers; the Fragment Society, 1812, to provide clothing and bedding for needy children; the Children's Friend Society, to provide day care for young children of working mothers; and a Penitent Females' Refuge, to help rescue and rehabilitate "those poor unhappy females who have wandered into the paths of vice and folly." [2] She also founded societies to minister to immigrants, blacks, and Jews. No wonder Mary Webb was described as a "society within herself."

Such unprecedented activity of women was not accomplished without opposition. Her physical condition and immense personal popularity probably shielded Miss Webb from much public criticism. However, she must have been aware that some felt the women were taking too much upon themselves. In one report she spoke of women as "destined by the Parent of nature to fill more retired stations in life than our brethren." Yet, she insisted, it is proper for women to organize and promote missions.[3] By 1819 this society had raised $3,825, of which Baptist members had given $2,200.[4] This may seem like a modest sum today but was substantial then. They had also corresponded with 210 other women's societies and helped unite women for prayer and missions.

Wadmalow and Edisto Society.—One cannot establish for certain the earliest women's missionary society in the South, but the one on Edisto Island off Charleston, South Carolina, must rank as one of the first. In 1807 Richard Furman, pastor in Charleston, visited Edisto Island and baptized a number of converts, black and white. From this evangelistic effort resulted a society of women from the two towns on the island, first known as the Wadmalow and Edisto Female Mite Society. The exact date of origin is unknown, but in 1812 an offering of $122.50 was reported for a school among the Catawba Indians. The group must have been formed at least by

1811 and possibly much earlier. This is often regarded as the first missionary society among Baptist women in the South.[5]

The leader of the Edisto Society was Mrs. Hepzibeth Jenkins Townsend, whose home was a central meeting place for the society. Her efforts also led to formation of a church on Edisto Island, attended by both whites and blacks.

One also sees the influence of Richard Furman, innovative pastor at Charleston. Before 1800 Furman had organized children of his church into a Juvenile Missionary and Education Society. This group provided Bible study, there being no Sunday Schools at that time, and also raised mission money to help educate young ministers and send missionaries to the nearby Catawba Indians.[6]

Hyco Female Cent Society.—Some think the Hyco Society in North Carolina was the earliest women's missionary society in the South. It probably dates from about 1810. As early as 1805 the Baptist Philanthropic Missionary Society was at work in North Carolina, working for "the elevation of the Indians." The Chowan Missionary Society was also quite early. Luther Rice organized mission societies at Edenton in 1817 and Raleigh in 1818.

Female Missionary Society of Richmond.—In 1813 the Baptist women of Richmond formed a society, having been directly influenced by Mary Webb of Boston. This society faced opposition from some of the men who feared what the women might do. The appeal of the men to the pastor to intervene met failure, however. The pastor said, "I never have heard of praying doing anybody any harm. . . . For my part the sisters may pray on." [7]

Female Missionary Society of Baltimore.—Baltimore was a strong center for Baptist work in the South and from early days was a strategic center for women's mission work. The Baptist women formed a society there in 1813. Among their early projects was making clothing for Cherokee children.

Other Societies.—From these early beginnings we see women's missionary societies springing up throughout the South. The earliest such society reported in Kentucky was 1822, though there had been a few children's mite societies before then. Georgia reported four missionary societies in 1817. When the Alabama Baptist state convention was formed in 1823, delegates from seven women's missionary societies participated. Arkansas dates missionary work from 1828 when a group of women from the Spring River area asked Reverend David Orr of Missouri to come to the territory. In 1835 Mrs. Sarah Hale gave the land and helped build a log church at the present site of Hot Springs. During times when no pastor was available, "Mrs. Hale would read the Scriptures and comment upon them."[8]

Texas Baptist women were active in missions from early days. In 1832 Baptist women formed the Thicket Prayer Meeting, so-called because the women met in thick woods from fear of Indians. Later this work achieved more definite organizational status. Among leaders were Mrs. Massie Millard and Mrs. Annette Bledsoe.

These societies appealed to women in the nineteenth century. They could combine sewing, social life, and missionary efforts. Many of the societies took a broad definition of "missions," including what today would be called social ministries. These societies also allowed the women to develop their awareness of themselves and the world, to learn what other women were doing in their own and other lands, and to hone their gifts for leadership. They also tended to prepare teachers for the Sunday Schools just then coming into existence throughout the South.

The Triennial Convention

Baptists in America quite early developed local associations and societies, but national organization was slow in coming. Many Baptists feared organization and sought to preserve their precious freedom by exaggerated independence. The churches were scattered and communication was a problem. No overwhelming cause arose to cause Baptists to come together in a national organization. However, early in the nineteenth century, missions proved the cause that would transform scattered churches into a tightknit denomination.

The conversion to Baptist views of Adoniram and Ann Judson, along with Luther Rice, was the catalyst that drew Baptists together. The Judsons and Rice were Congregationalists, appointed missionaries to India in 1812. On the ship voyage the Judsons spent time studying the Greek New Testament. They knew the venerable old Baptist missionary, William Carey, would meet them and they would have to give account of their faith. While studying the New Testament, Adoniram Judson was dismayed to discover that the Baptists were correct in their views of baptism. Ann at first greatly resisted these views, but at length both were convinced and in India received immersion as Baptists. Luther Rice, who came a few weeks later by a different ship, reached a similar decision.

Of course, integrity required the young people to resign from the Congregational board, which left them in India without sponsorship. Carey wrote immediately to the Baptists in Boston, explaining the situation. He offered to support the Americans through the English Baptist Mission, but suggested it would be far better if the Americans would support them. Dr. Thomas C. Baldwin, Mary Webb's pastor, agreed to help enlist Baptist support. Miss Webb's society immediately directed some of its offerings to the Judsons.

In addition, Luther Rice agreed to come back to America to "stir up the Baptists" to missionary support. He intended this to be just a brief time, prior to returning to India. Instead, he spent the remainder of his fruitful life in this task and never returned to the foreign field. His valuable leadership among the Baptists helped countless others to go as foreign missionaries.

On May 18, 1814, 26 ministers and 7 laymen from 11 states and the District of Columbia met in Philadelphia and formed a new Baptist organization. They adopted the cumbersome name of "The General Convention of the Baptist Denomination in the United States of America for Foreign Missions." However, since this body was to meet only every three years, it was popularly called the Triennial Convention.

This was the first Baptist body in America with national scope. It was formed primarily as a foreign mission society, particularly to sponsor the Judsons. However, this body later was expanded to include home missions, Christian education, and Christian publications. One of its first actions was to appoint Luther Rice as "general agent," to travel among the churches and enlist support for missions.

While no women were present at the 1814 formation, some of the men represented women's societies. At the second meeting, in 1817, reports indicate that there were at least 187 known Baptist missionary societies in the nation, 110 of them women's societies. Membership in the Triennial Convention was based upon financial contribution to missions, and delegates might come from churches or mission societies. The women's societies were always represented by men. Most of these societies had started for home missions, but after 1814 they included foreign missions in their work.

Women made a significant contribution to the Triennial Convention. The very first contribution to that body was from a woman, in the amount of $50. Baptist women first had the vision of foreign missions, and women had also shown that people would contribute to the support of missions.

Two women appointed to foreign fields by the Triennial Convention captured the imagination of Baptist women and multiplied their missionary zeal. These were Ann Judson and Henrietta Hall Shuck. The Judsons, who were already in India, were adopted by the Triennial Convention in 1814. The Shucks were appointed to China in 1835.

Ann, the beautiful daughter of Deacon John Hasseltine, grew up without a care. As a youth perhaps her major concern was what frock to wear on an outing up the Merrimac. At the age of 20, she married Adoniram Judson, a young ministerial student who had applied for appointment as a foreign missionary. Her parents never approved this union but did not prevent it.

In Burma, where the Judsons went from India, Ann found herself far more than just a missionary wife and mother. She had access to the Burmese homes, as her husband did not, and soon found herself totally involved in sharing the gospel. The story of her incredible courage and heroism while her husband was in prison is well-known. Without doubt she saved his life and also saved the mission work.

However, perhaps Ann Judson's greatest impact for missions was made in this country. She was a prodigious letter writer, and her letters were passed around and read by dozens of women's mission societies. Her vivid and detailed descriptions of daily life in Burma, the moral and spiritual degradation, and her appeal for aid fell on eager ears in America. "Ann of Ava" became a legend in her own time and gave Baptist women a heroine and role model of their own.

Henrietta Hall grew up in a privileged Virginia family, and later married J. Lewis Shuck. He was committed to foreign missions. At a mission rally an offering was being received, and young Shuck had no money. He wrote on a slip of paper, "I give myself," and dropped that in the offering plate. In 1835 he and his new bride sailed for China.

Beautiful, cultured, and charming, Henrietta Shuck was a woman of influence. In China she conducted a school for girls, in addition to caring for her own household of husband and four children. Somehow she found time to write letters to Southern Baptist women, letters which had a powerful impact. Henrietta Shuck was a powerful missionary influence in the South before Lottie Moon was born. If anything, her premature death in 1845 tended to solidify her place in the hearts of Baptist women in the South.

The first single woman applied for appointment to the Triennial Convention in 1815. She was Charlotte H. White, a widow, who had long felt a call to missions. Knowing the board would not send out a woman alone, Mrs. White asked to be attached to the family of Mr. and Mrs. George Hough, who had recently been appointed to India. She wrote that "My wishes are to reside in their family in the character of a sister to Mrs. Hough and a sister in the Lord; with them to pursue such studies as are requisite to the discharge of missionary duties." [9] Mrs. White offered: "to apply what talents I possess wholly to the service of the mission, either in taking the management of a school, or to hold private meetings, should there be an opportunity, with native females, to instruct them in the principles of the gospel, hoping, by the blessing of God, that some of them will be raised from their degraded and miserable condition, to participate in the riches of salvation." [10]

This passage not only reveals the dedication of Mrs. White, but also something of the duties of women missionaries at that time. The board was favorable to Mrs. White's request. At that time society allowed a widow far more freedom than an unmarried single woman, since presumably the widow had been long enough under the guidance of a husband to gain some stability. Besides, Mrs. White offered to outfit herself and give all the remainder of her possessions to the Convention. She was appointed and sailed with the Houghs in December, 1815.

However, within a few weeks Mrs. White's plans changed dramatically. The Americans resided for some weeks with William Carey at the English Baptist mission in Serampore. One of the English

Baptist missionaries was Joshua Rowe, a single man. He and Mrs. White were soon married, and went to an important new station at Digha where they established a most successful work. She continued in missionary service after Mr. Rowe's death. Because they had incurred no expense, the Triennial Convention refunded her contribution. William Carey was well impressed with her, for he wrote, "I consider her marriage as a very providential circumstance. At Digha she cannot fail of being useful." [11]

Adoniram Judson was apparently much relieved by this marriage. In a frank letter to Lucius Bolles, marked "private," Judson said somewhat ungallantly: "Mrs. White very fortunately disposed of herself in Bengal. Fortunately, I say; for I know not how we would have disposed of her in this place. We do not apprehend that the mission of single females to such a country as Burmah, is at all advisable." [12]

This hardly fits with Judson's previous letter that shiploads of women could be used in missions, but it does reflect practical problems in Burma. When a single woman lived in a missionary family, no amount of explanation could have avoided the impression of polygamy. It seemed not to dawn upon Convention leaders that single women could live separately.

The first unmarried single women were appointed by Baptists in 1832. In that year Sarah Cummings and Caroline Harrington were sent to Burma.

Four years later Eleanor Macomber was appointed to work among the Karen people of Burma. She went far beyond the traditional role of a woman missionary. She insisted on living alone in the native village of Dong Yhan, and became an effective evangelist, teacher, and church builder. Her appointment and her innovative role aroused some opposition. Some expressed dismay that a young woman would be appointed "with no strong arm to lean on." Even if she could live in physical safety, some said, how could a single woman possibly cope with important decisions without a man to help?

The same year that Miss Macomber was appointed, the respected Dr. Rufus Anderson said: "It has been urged upon missionary societies to send out unmarried females. . . . Few however appear to be aware of the difficulties of placing the single female in circumstances to live and labor happily in pagan lands." [13]

His conclusion, to which most Baptists would probably have agreed, was "that unmarried females should rarely be sent on missions."

Miss Macomber won numerous converts, some of whom were baptized by Adoniram Judson. Given his views of women missionaries, one can only surmise his reactions. Miss Macomber died at the age of 39 of an attack of what was then called "jungle fever."

Southern Baptist Women (1845–1888)

No women are listed among the delegates who formed the Southern Baptist Convention in Augusta, Georgia, in 1845, though some of the men there represented women's societies. The two major issues over which Baptists, North and South, split asunder were the abolition controversy and a disagreement over mission work. Baptist women had been prime movers in abolitionism. They had also led out in the mission movement, especially in the South, and had already shown unmistakably the viability of organization for that purpose.

The Rise of Missionary Organizations.—The earliest general meeting of Southern Baptist women was in Baltimore in 1868. A number of women, mostly wives attending the Southern Baptist Convention with their husbands, gathered at the home of Mrs. Ann Graves. She read to the assembled ladies some letters from her son Rosewell, a Southern Baptist missionary in China. His letters described the need for women missionaries to penetrate the "culture curtain" and reach Chinese women for Christ.

After 1868 Southern Baptist women continued to meet at the time of the Convention. Interest mushroomed and organizations multiplied at the local church level. In 1872 the SBC took its first recorded notice of the women's work when it asked the Foreign Mission Board to include in its report a section on the work of "Bible women." This probably reflected the attitude of H. A. Tupper, secretary of the Board, who was an early and consistent friend of the women's mission work.

The committee to whom this report was referred reported, "We also respectfully, but earnestly, urge upon the delegates present to take immediate steps to organize Female Missionary Societies in their churches. Select some active, pious woman, who will assemble the sisters together, and organize them for the purpose of cultivating the missionary spirit and systematic contributions." [14]

Already the womens' societies were proving their value, so the Convention urged that "the sisterhood of our Southern Zion should be aroused" to missions. Thereafter a report on "Woman's Work" was a fairly regular feature of the SBC program, usually in connection with the report of the Foreign Board and always given by a man.

The hundreds of local church societies had little correlation, however, until the formation of a Central Committee of Baptist women in each state, beginning with South Carolina in 1876. Even before that, strong local organizations, such as those in Richmond and Baltimore, provided a kind of statewide leadership. Local societies were encouraged to report their work to the state Central Committee, which would formulate a national report.

Some societies also sent contributions to the state group, who in turn divided them out to the various causes. This came rather close to the pattern of separate organization which characterized women in other denominations. The Baptist women could have, though they did not, appoint their own missionaries. They did channel much of their support to "female missionaries" in China.

Many Southern Baptist men feared the women would form separate mission boards, as women of most other denominations had done, though the women repeatedly assured them they had no such separationist intentions. Lottie Moon, who helped shape the women's work from half a world away, wrote: "What we want is not power. . . . Power of appointment and of disbursing of funds should be left, as heretofore, in the hands of the Foreign Mission Board. Separate organization is undesirable, and would do harm; but organization in subordination to the Board is the imperative need of the hour." [15]

The issue was settled in 1888 when delegates from several of the state Central Committees met in Richmond and formed the Woman's Missionary Union, Auxiliary to the Southern Baptist Convention. The body was not officially a part of the Convention, but neither was it entirely separate. To this day the WMU has supported denominational causes, rather than sponsoring its own separate missionary programs.

It is amazing to see how quickly the women's societies established themselves as a basic part of SBC work. Convention reports are clear that what was almost an afterthought in the 1870's became the backbone of Southern Baptist missions by 1880's. In an understatement, the 1889 Convention admitted that women were rapidly "becoming one of the most fruitful sources of missionary influence and income." [16]

However, the women's work created some rivalry. In 1880 the Home Mission Board complained that it was not receiving its fair share of support from the women. The next year that Board expressed the hope "that the cooperation of the women of our churches, which has proved so efficient upon other fields of Christian effort, shall not be withheld from us in our endeavors to evangelize our own people." [17] In 1882 there were an estimated 500 women's missionary societies among Southern Baptists. Of these, over 350 contributed to the Foreign Board, while only 31 contributed to the Home Board. [18] Perhaps the uncertain future of the Home Mission Board just then was a factor.

Various efforts were made to work out a plan whereby both Boards could share in the women's work. One cannot escape the impression from the records that the Foreign Board dragged its feet, perhaps feeling that women's work should be confined to foreign missions. Almost like two suitors, the two Boards vied for the support of Southern Baptist women. In 1877 there was a suggestion to form *two* central committees in each state, one for each Board, but this was never widely implemented.

The women were not quick to decide, apparently realizing their position of strength. Their freedom of choice is reflected in the action of the Ladies Society of First Baptist Church of Dallas. In 1891 members listened politely to Dr. J. B. Cranfill, then head of home mission work in Texas. Immediately after his fervent plea for home missions, the women appropriated every penny in their treasury— to *foreign* missions! [19] Such freedom of choice contributed to the growing influence of Baptist women, who could not easily be ignored, much less opposed.

Even before formation of WMU the women had decided to support the total denominational program. The Home Board reported in 1886 that "The Board is under special obligation to the sisterhood composing these Societies for their efforts and generous contributions to its work . . . . We are gratified to know that these societies, almost without exception, have resolved to limit themselves to no one department of Christian missions, but to share with their brothers in the support of every enterprise fostered by the denomination." [20] An 1895 report says the women "labor for no one Board, but for the Convention, and so all three of our Boards receive the same cordial co-operation." [21] However, as late as 1931 when the SBC was bogged down in debt, it took special pleading by Convention leaders to persuade the WMU to help pay off the entire Convention debt, rather than channel all help to the Foreign Mission Board.

The first proposal for a significant SBC leadership role for women came in 1882. In that year the Convention authorized the Boards to appoint "some competent woman as Superintendent of the State Central Committees, whose duty it shall be to collect and disseminate information and in other ways to stimulate and strengthen woman's work for women in all lands." [22] The Foreign Board, however, was hesitant to act on what it called "a difficult and delicate problem." It felt that since "a false step now might entail fatal embarrassments for years to come, we have chosen to move slowly and cautiously." [23] It apparently feared that Southern Baptist women might form separate organizations, as other church women had, and that additional leadership of women might alienate Southern Baptists who were acutely aware of the controversial suffrage movement of the times.

Southern Baptist women thus failed in their first bid for a significant leadership role in the SBC, for no such woman superintendent was ever appointed. Such a woman would have been salaried, would have traveled widely among the churches, and no doubt would have had many opportunities to speak. Such a leadership post might have altered the shape of the women's work to the present time.

Woman's Missionary Union, and the various local and state organizations which preceded it, must be interpreted in context. More than missions was involved. Southern Baptist women were acutely aware and interested in the struggle for women's rights. Their church societies represented a kind of freedom expression of their own. It gave them a chance for organization, for leadership, for combining their energies and voices for causes in which they believed.

Many of the men opposed the women's work precisely because they perceived it to be related to or at least similar to the women's rights movement. Some of the women showed definite liberationist tendencies. As early as 1885 some Baptist women voted to restrict their meetings to women only. When requested to allow a man to write their reports, the women replied cooly that "this is a Woman's Missionary Union, and there is no need for gentlemen to frame our resolutions." [24]

It is well-known that whereas organizations for women, such as WMU, flourish, similar organizations for men tend to languish. This seems equally true in most denominations. Perhaps the major reason is that women's organizations provided a necessary outlet for women's ideas and leadership. The men did not need any such auxiliary because they were running the whole church.

Even before the formation of WMU in 1888, the women's societies had opened up new opportunities of service to Southern Baptist women. Many of the state Baptist papers began to carry columns, or even entire pages, under such titles as "The Women's Work." Some of these would be considered demeaning today, but at least they allowed women an opportunity for writing. Women also wrote and published magazines of their own, such as *The Heathen Helper* and *The Baptist Basket*. The *Foreign Mission Journal* and *Kind Words* also gave an opportunity for women to express themselves. Also in 1891, before formation of the present Sunday School Board, it was reported that the women's "leaflet literature" was flourishing. [25]

Women pioneered many ways in mission work before 1888. Their emphasis upon *regular* offerings, however small, and preferably given on the Lord's Day, is a forerunner of Southern Baptist stewardship patterns to this day. The little "mite boxes," containers for the offerings at home, paved the way for the offering envelopes of today.

Women also pioneered in the creation of missionary literature. Their leaflets, Bible study lessons, news about what others were doing, missionary testimonies, and above all, letters from the mission field, set the standard for mission literature. In some states the women were assigned a column in the state Baptist paper. In other places, like Baltimore, the Baptist women launched a viable literature operation in which they wrote, published, and distributed missionary materials.

Perhaps the greatest examples of mission literature centered in two Kentucky papers. *The Heathen Helper* was launched in 1882 by the Central Committee of Kentucky, with other states invited to appoint a "contributing editress." Edited by Agnes Osborne, this attractive eight-page paper was called "a worthy sister of the *Foreign Missionary Journal.*" [26]

Somewhat later *The Baptist Basket* made its appearance, also in Kentucky, edited by Mrs. Thomas Osborne. Well-written and with a great deal of human interest material, *The Baptist Basket* lasted longer and looked as if it might become a national Baptist woman's magazine. In addition to missionary stories and letters, it stressed tithing as the biblical plan of stewardship, an idea foreign to most Baptists at that time.

Lottie Moon

No account of Southern Baptist foreign missions would be complete without some notice of Charlotte Diggs Moon, appointed as a single woman missionary to China in 1873. If Mary Webb was the pioneer to first arouse Baptist women to missions, perhaps Lottie Moon had done more to inspire, encourage, and channel the energies of Southern Baptist women than any other person.

Born in 1840 into a privileged Virginia family, Lottie Moon had at first no intention of becoming a missionary. As a child she was quite uninterested in church, but was soundly converted at the age of 16. Lottie was a brilliant girl and had the good fortune to be born into a family that believed its daughters as well as sons should be educated. She attended the finest schools of the day and proved an outstanding student.

Three of the Moon girls eventually became foreign missionaries, but only Lottie remained for life. Her older sister Orianne was one of the first women physicians in America and served for a time as a medical missionary in Jerusalem under the Disciples of Christ. Her younger sister, Edmonia, was appointed to China by the Foreign Mission Board in 1872. Many think this was a major influence in Lottie's decision to go to China.

Passing up all opportunities to marry, Lottie left Virginia after the death of her parents and moved to Cartersville, Georgia, where she conducted a fashionable girls' school. In the spring of 1873 her pastor preached a moving missionary sermon. At its conclusion Lottie Moon went forward, and said, "I have long known that God wants me in China." A few weeks later, with minimal training and preparation, she was on her way.

In China, Lottie's first disappointment was Edmonia's illness. The rigors of China had been hard on Edmonia, not yet twenty years old. She was a victim of deep and debilitating depression, a problem pervasive in the Moon family, from which Lottie herself was not entirely free. As Edmonia became unable to function, Lottie brought her home to Virginia and returned to China alone.

Miss Moon learned the Chinese language in the household of Reverend and Mrs. T. P. Crawford, veteran but eccentric Southern Baptist missionaries to China. Crawford later broke with Southern Baptists and sought to dismantle the Foreign Mission Board. How much of his "independent" ideas Lottie Moon absorbed is conjecture, but it is interesting that she frequently had sharp criticism for the Board and at least once offered to resign.

Established at Pingtu in North China, Miss Moon began a gruelling regimen that lasted year after year. She kept a school for girls, traveled to neighboring villages to teach and distribute Bibles, and spoke with Chinese women wherever she could. Traveling to remote villages by rickshaw, Miss Moon would gather a crowd however she could and then read from the Bible and tell them about Jesus Christ. Some of the men missionaries complained that Lottie Moon was preaching, a charge which incensed her. She replied that the people needed and wanted to hear of Christ, and if the men did not like the way she was sharing the gospel, let them send some men to do it better. Perhaps she would have agreed with the woman who felt that while she was not ordained to preach, she was foreordained.

Were Lottie Moon here today there is no doubt she would be in the forefront of the struggle for women's leadership roles in the church. She amazed and sometimes offended male missionaries by refusing to accept the traditional silent role of the woman missionary in mission meetings. Instead, she insisted upon taking a full share in the discussion and decision regarding any mission policy.

Great as was her impact in China, Lottie Moon's greatest impact was in this country. On her occasional furloughs, she traveled around the country speaking at countless gatherings, mostly to women. An engaging personality and powerful speaker, Moon inspired Southern Baptist women to greater involvement in missions. In addition to her visits, her frequent letters home were read and reread by countless Baptist women and helped shape Southern Baptist work from half a world away.

Lottie Moon constantly urged greater organization for Southern Baptist women, pointing to the example of women among Methodists and Presbyterians. Citing the advantages of organization of women in those denominations, she wrote in 1887: "Until the women of our Southern Baptist churches are thoroughly aroused, we shall continue to go on in our present hand-to-mouth system. . . . I am convinced that one of the chief reasons our Southern Baptist women do so little is the lack of organization." [27]

It was Lottie Moon who first suggested a special Christmas offering for missions, certainly with no idea that it would ever bear her name.

After 1900 Miss Moon became more frail, but kept up her incredible work schedule. She suffered both physically and emotionally during the Boxer Rebellion of 1912, a radical revolution in China which some compare to the Red Guard of more recent times. Food was scarce, and Moon agonized for the welfare of the Chinese girls of her school. Ignoring repeated pleas of the Board that she come home, the seventy-two year old Moon kept at her job. Not until later was it known that she starved herself in order to share more food with her beloved girls. While the famine was serious, apparently literal starvation was not imminent. If part of the crisis was in her own imagination, that does not detract from her heroism and love in denying herself for others.

Finally the Board sent a registered nurse, Cynthia Miller, to China to escort Miss Moon home. Aged and frail, Moon died off the coast of Japan on December 24, 1912. Cremated in accordance to Japanese law, her ashes were later interred in Virginia, where the Baptist women erected a monument at her grave. Her name, the dates 1840-1912, and these words appear there: "Forty years a missionary of the Southern Baptist Convention in China. Faithful unto death."

There is literally no way to calculate the impact this women had upon Southern Baptist missions. Through her example and words, millions of Baptist women and men have been informed, inspired, challenged, and directed into useful participation in sharing the gospel around the world.

Woman's Missionary Union, 1888

Between 1868 and 1872 the women in most major denominations formed national organizations for missions. Most of these were separate groups in which the women raised their own funds and appointed their own missionaries separately from the denomination. The Civil War had brought abolition, which had been for two generations a primary goal of women's reforming zeal. The rapidly expanding missionary work gave churchwomen a cause that was genuinely religious, and also with significant social and humanitarian dimensions. Missions rapidly replaced abolition as the primary focus of the women's movement.

While much caught up in the missionary cause, Southern Baptist women did not achieve national organization until 1888. At first their local societies had little close contact with other such groups, and sharing of information and development of a common approach were hindered. However, Southern Baptist women were aware of what other women were doing. A national organization was just a matter of time. By the mid-1870s the work of most of the local societies was correlated at the state level by the Central Committees, and in 1888 the formation of Woman's Missionary Union completed the national structure.

Several factors help account for this delay, none of them being lack of missionary interest and zeal. Baptist women in the South were probably more conservative socially at this time, and many of them were not yet sure how far women should go in organizing and speaking out even for such a worthy cause as missions. They were also sensitive to opposition from many Southern Baptists who feared the women would harm the Convention.

Perhaps the main cause for delay was uncertainty about what kind of structure to form. Unlike their sisters in other denominations, Southern Baptist women preferred to work within the established mission boards. In the twenty years between 1868-1888 they resisted extremist views on the one hand that they should remain silent, and on the other that they should bolt the denomination and form their own separate group. By 1888 they had devised a unique plan by which Southern Baptist women could pursue their own work in their own way and yet be loyally related to the Southern Baptist Convention as an auxiliary.

The first step to the national organization was formation of a Central Committee in each state. Dr. H. A. Tupper, long a friend of the women's work, was convinced by 1874 that there was need for more correlation of the societies. He arranged for the appointment of the mission society of the Welsh Neck Church as the Central Committee for South Carolina, with Martha McIntosh as chairman. Minutes of the Welsh Neck Society record the following response: "1875. Sabbath morning, January 10th. A special meeting of the Society was held after service to consider a proposition . . . that our Society act as a Central Committee with Miss M. E. McIntosh as chairman, to arouse an interest in this work among the women of our State and secure contributions. The proposition was assented to unanimously." [28]

This was an important step forward in structuring the women's work. Other states followed until most had Central Committees to promote, correlate, and record the women's work in missions.

Part of the work of the Central Committee was to encourage formation of local missionary societies in places that did not have them. In 1876 E. T. Winkler, chairman of Woman's Work Committee of the SBC, reported: "We think it would be a good plan to establish a female missionary society in every church which all the ladies should be invited to join. A monthly meeting encouraged by the pastor and an annual meeting with special services would nourish its vitality." [29]

However, not all Southern Baptists favored these developments. Some feared the women's work would get out of hand and move in the direction of the suffragettes. Others feared they would divide the convention. Frankly, some feared the women would overemphasize missions to the neglect of other worthy causes. To this fear Tupper replied that so long as the combined efforts of men and women fell so far short of missionary needs, it would be better to stimulate the men to greater effort than to restrain the women.

At the conclusion of the 1877 report of the Committee on Women's Work, A. T. Spalding said: "The time may be at hand when it will be advisable that they shall appoint a Central Committee to combine their efforts, to stimulate the work, and to give permanent record to their success." [30] This was the first vague suggestion for some overall organization to correlate the work of Baptist women in the several states, but it bore no fruit for another decade.

In 1884 there was a meeting of women from various Central Committees held during the Southern Baptist Convention. At this meeting there was specific conversation about the possibility of effecting a more definite national organization. There was some carry-over, for in 1889 the 1884 meeting was referred to as the sixth annual meeting.

Clearly the stage was set for organization. At the 1887 meeting of women in Louisville, Kentucky, Miss Annie Armstrong of Baltimore introduced the following resolution:

> 1. *Resolved,* That a committee be appointed to request Central Committees of the several States, each to appoint three lady delegates, to meet during the next session of the Southern Baptist Convention, to decide upon the advisability of organizing a general committee; and if advisable to provide for the appointment, location and duties thereof.

> 2. *Resolved,* That the above is not to be construed as a desire, upon the part of the ladies, to interfere with the management of the existing Boards of the Convention, either in the appointment of missionaries, or the direction of mission work; but is a desire, on their part, to be more efficient in collecting money and disseminating information on mission subjects. [32]

The caution expressed in the second part of the resolution was fully justified. Some leaders of the mission boards were apprehensive. The editor of the *Foreign Mission Journal* wrote: "We shall watch the progress of this movement with no little interest, sympathizing with every aspiration of our women after better doing for the Master, yet earnestly hoping and striving against any effort that may come to be made to effect a separation of woman's work from that of our Convention. The trend of affairs in other religious bodies is in the direction of this independent woman's work. Let us hope that through the wide conservatism of our people, both men and women, this independence may never obtain among us. It can be avoided by the Convention's giving proper recognition to this work and allowing to it such representation upon the floor of the body as will not conflict with the constitution of the body nor with the sentiments of our people in regard to woman's true position in this work." [33]

The refusal of the Convention in its 1885 session to seat women as messengers was probably an added stimulus toward organization for women. From 1868 the women had sought a way to work cooperatively within the Convention. When that body changed its constitution in 1885 to exclude women as messengers, many feared with good reason, that this could provoke the kind of separation they had sought to avoid.

The real leader behind the 1888 organization was Annie Armstrong of Baltimore. Long active in local missionary societies, Armstrong was in correspondence with Lottie Moon of China. Both were strong-minded women, and both were convinced that only by organization could the resources of Southern Baptist women be channeled into mission work.

In May of 1888 a group of Southern Baptist women met at the Broad Street Methodist Church in Richmond, Virginia, hard by the meeting site of the Southern Baptist Convention. Unlike many similar meetings in the past, these women were official delegates from their state Central Committees, appointed specifically to consider forming a national organization. In an opening devotional, F. M. Ellis of Baltimore said: "If you know what to do, go ahead and do it; if not, take more time, but more time is losing time. I hope this meeting will result in immediate organization, thus helping to train the women and children to Christianize the great Southland." [34]

Martha McIntosh of South Carolina presided at this crucial meeting. Indeed most of the women knew what they wanted to do, but some were reluctant. Fannie Stout of South Carolina and a close friend of McIntosh addressed the group. She said: "The question of organization of Southern Baptist women for mission work has been exciting thought and discussion for years." Even the men, she said, considered it one of the most pressing questions of the hour. She then detailed benefits which would come from such organization, concluding: "We organize simply for greater efficiency in work and our work is the work of the Convention. We do not desire a separate work, but if in some particulars we separate ourselves as women, it is that we may gather greater momentum with which to push forward our united work." [35]

In a statement that could only have been aimed at opposition to women organizing, Stout said the women had found nothing in the Bible to forbid them to organize, to work among women, and to teach other women the Word of God. In a cautious vein, she said: "Much will depend on the spirit which we show. The brethren are our guardians—and when they realize what we want to do, that we do not wish to wander in any dangerous ways, but are only trying to follow them as our leaders and trying to carry into practice what they have taught us from pulpit and press, their anxieties will cease." [36]

After this moving speech, Armstrong immediately moved to consider organization. Ten states favored; North Carolina was not represented, Mississippi passed, and Virginia, host for the meeting, had to wait for approval of the men. By a compromise the vote was postponed until May 14, when delegates from ten states overwhelmingly voted to organize and adopt a constitution. Only Mississippi and Virginia refused, and their concern was more procedural than substantive.

Martha McIntosh was named president, and Annie Armstrong was named Corresponding Secretary, with headquarters at Baltimore. The constitution adopted in 1888 was primarily the work of Annie and Alice Armstrong. The name chosen was Woman's Missionary Union, Auxiliary to the Southern Baptist Convention. A similar name had been in use in Texas since 1880.

Annie Armstrong served as Corresponding Secretary from 1888 to 1906, without salary. Elected at the age of 38, she brought to her task excellent training, wide experience in missionary society work, and a progressive spirit expressed by her favorite motto, "Go Forward." Sometimes irascible and quick-tempered, Armstrong was also a woman of wisdom and leadership. The first headquarters was an upper room provided rent free by the Maryland Baptist Union Association. Since 1886 this "Mission Room" had served as a combination office, library, and reading room for the women's missionary societies of Baltimore, and it was natural that Armstrong should continue to work there.

Baptist Women and Missions Today

While not a history of Woman's Missionary Union as such, this chapter must take account of the missionary work of women since

1888. Through their promotion, literature, and offerings, women have educated, inspired, and enlisted Southern Baptists into missionary work. Perhaps the women are largely responsible for making the Southern Baptist Convention one of the most missionary-minded of all modern denominations.

One way Southern Baptist women have stimulated missions is by special offerings. Each spring Southern Baptist churches receive the Annie Armstrong Offering for Home Missions and late each fall they receive the Lottie Moon Offering for Foreign Missions. The first special offering for foreign missions was given in 1888. Lottie Moon wrote suggesting that Southern Baptist women set a week of special prayer for foreign missions and also promote a special offering. She suggested the week before Christmas be set aside for this purpose. She said: "Need it be said why the week before Christmas is chosen? Is it not the festive season, when families and friends exhange gifts in memory of the Gift laid on the altar of the world for the redemption of the human race, the most appropriate time to consecrate a portion from both abounding riches and scant poverty to send forth the good tidings of great joy into all the earth?" [37]

The original purpose was to raise money for a woman missionary to assist Moon and specifically to provide a replacement so she could have a long-delayed furlough. Armstrong was impressed by these letters from Lottie Moon and determined that her three-month-old organization would try to help. In a letter to Tupper of the Foreign Board, she asked, "Dare we spend $100 for literature? Would the reckless expenditure of postage be justified by the results?"

Tupper encouraged her to proceed, and the Board provided the $100 for postage and promotion. It was one of the best investments the Board ever made. The first goal was $2,000, which few thought could be reached. However, total receipts were almost $3,300. This offering has been an annual event in Southern Baptist churches since 1888. Annie Armstrong suggested it bear the name of Lottie Moon, and in 1918 the WMU adopted the name "Lottie Moon Christmas Offering for Foreign Missions." In the 1960's there were suggestions to change the name because some feared too much was being made of one missionary, Lottie Moon. However, the name remains.

From that small beginning the Lottie Moon offering has grown. At first it was primarily an offering from Baptist women, but for most churches after World War II, it became a church-wide campaign. In 1977 total receipts from this offering were well in excess of $30 million.

In 1894 the Union voted to observe a "Week of Self-Denial" to increase gifts to missions. In 1895, due to a plea from I. T. Tichenor of the Home Board, that week was set apart as a time of prayer and contributions to Home Missions. From that time the Week of Self-Denial continued to be devoted to home mission needs as the Christmas offering was devoted to foreign missions. In 1922 the name was changed to "Thank-offering," and in 1933 it was renamed the "Annie W. Armstrong Offering for Home Missions." The 1977 offering for this purpose was over $9 million.

No cause has so awakened Baptist women as missions. From earliest times they have organized, taught, and given money to send the gospel to others. No account of the role of Baptist women today could possibly overlook their work in missions, where they first learned to plan and carry out their own denominational programs.

Notes

[1] Albert L. Vail, *Mary Webb and the Mother Society* (Philadelphia: American Baptist Publication Society, 1914), ii.

[2] Ibid., 64.   [3] Ibid., 45.

[4] Helen Falls, "Baptist Women in Missions Support in the Nineteenth Century," *Baptist History and Heritage* (January, 1977), 27.

[5] Ethlene Boone Cox, *Following in His Train* (Nashville: Broadman Press, 1938), 34.

[6] Ibid., 33.

[7] Alma Hunt, *History of Woman's Missionary Union* (Nashville: Convention Press, 1964), 8.

[8] Cox, 36.

[9] R. Pierce Beaver, *All Loves Excelling: American Protestant Women in World Missions* (Grand Rapids: William B. Eerdmans, 1968), 64.

[10] Ibid.   [11] Ibid., 66.   [12] Ibid.

[13] Ibid., 61.

[14] *SBC Annual,* 1872, 14, 35.

[15] Hunt, 24.

[16] *SBC Annual,* 1889, III Appendix A.

[17] *SBC Annual,* 1881, 61–62.

[18] *SBC Annual,* 1882, 25.

[19] Leon McBeth, *The First Baptist Church of Dallas 1868-1968* (Grand Rapids: Zondervan Publishing House, 1968), 106.

[20] *SBC Annual,* 1886, VIII, Appendix A.
[21] *SBC Annual,* 1895, 44.
[22] *SBC Annual,* 1882, 25.
[23] *SBC Annual,* 1882, 54.
[24] Hunt, 21, 49.
[25] *SBC Annual,* 1891, III, Appendix A.

[26] Hunt, 23.   [27] Ibid., 24.   [28] Ibid., 15.
[29] Ibid., 15-16.   [30] Ibid., 16.   [31] Ibid., 24.
[32] Ibid., 25.   [33] Ibid.   [34] Ibid., 27.
[35] Ibid., 29.   [36] Ibid., 30.

[37] Una Roberts Lawrence, *Lottie Moon* (Nashville: The Sunday School Board of the Southern Baptist Convention, 1927), 152-53.

FIVE

Women Seeking a Role

Nineteenth Century

Lucinda Williams wrapped her three-month-old baby against the December cold and went to speak to the landlady. Twenty-three-year-old Lucinda with her husband and baby, had just moved to town and did not know anyone yet. But it was Sunday, and Lucinda wanted to go to church. Back in Missouri both she and her lawyer husband had been devout Baptists. Surely the landlady, a Methodist, could direct them to the Baptist church.

To Lucinda's question the landlady replied that there was no Baptist church in town, and she hoped there never would be one. However, she had not calculated on the determination of the beautiful and talented Lou Williams. She replied quietly, "I am very sorry, Mrs. Moore, to hear you say that. I am a Baptist, and if I am to live here I want a Baptist church here." The landlady might have told her young tenant that three Baptist churches had been launched in this hostile climate, but none survived.

With her husband, Lou Williams determined to see a Baptist church started. It was her effort, largely, that resulted in the meeting of eight women and three men on July 30, 1868, to form a Baptist church. Until the church got on its feet, Lucinda, along with her husband Will, helped keep the church in existence. She helped form its first Sunday School. She led its first woman's missionary society. In its infant years the church had no building, and seemed likely to go the way of all its predecessors. But Lucinda Williams simply refused to allow the church to die. She roused the ladies of the church to help raise funds to build their own building. In 1873 the women, led by Mrs. Williams, raised over $600 toward the first building. While not enough to build, it was enough to start, and more importantly, it convinced the men that the women meant business.

Thus by 1873 the church had its own building. The church was growing; it had a growing Sunday School and an assured future. Much of this success was due to the beautiful, charming, and talented Lucinda Williams who simply would not give up. This church is still in existence today. In fact, it is the largest Southern Baptist church in the world, the First Baptist Church of Dallas, Texas.[1]

This example shows that Southern Baptist women were involved in more than missions. It would be a serious historical mistake to assume that the work of women was limited to missions alone. Rather, the evidence suggests that Baptist women were involved with the total life of the church. While they did not earn or control a great deal of money, or participate openly in church business decisions, Baptist women were influential beyond what most people today realize. To an extent that might surprise some, women have helped shape Southern Baptist churches and their programs and practices to this day.

In this chapter we will examine the historical evidence to see how women have influenced the local church, its stewardship, religious education, and other practices. We will also review the status of women in the Southern Baptist Convention in the nineteenth century, and review some of the attitudes toward women and their work at that time.

Women and the Local Church

The role of women in the Convention and in the missionary societies must not obscure their role in the local churches. Indeed, their major contributions were at the local church level. Probably from the first, women have made up the majority of Southern Baptist church members. By 1885 it was estimated that 60 percent of the one million Southern Baptists were women.[2] While that figure may have changed some since then, most would agree that women make up between 55 percent and 60 percent of Baptist membership today. In many churches they make up the majority of attenders, teachers, and workers of all kinds.

In the devastating days during and following the Civil War many Southern Baptist churches would not have survived without the women. On December 14, 1864, the *Confederate Baptist* reported that the war was bringing crisis to Baptist churches. The editor said: "The crisis is gradually depleting the male population at home; and if the stern measures of conscription enacted by our Legislature is pushed to its utmost limits, none but old men and boys will be left at home. Our deacons and Sunday School teachers, perhaps (tell it not in Gath) our ministers, may be turned into soldiers, and the churches left destitute of men to conduct their usual operations. Our women will have to take their places, and do what they can to sustain the institutions of religion. Already, we hear of female superintendents of Sunday Schools; and we know of some sisters, who although without official rank, are yet doing good service as deacons, by looking after the temporal affairs of their churches." [3]

This same editor later wrote: "We received a letter from a young sister, conveying a call from church, to supply preaching. We suppose that the male members are away, and the sisters have resolved to have public worship continued. We trust many will imitate this good example." [4]

From this and countless examples like it, we see that the women helped sustain the churches during the dark days of the war and its aftermath. This was true at the historic First Baptist Church of Nashville, Tennessee, where women kept the church going during the difficult days when the pastor was sometimes the only man present at the services. [5]

Stories are not lacking of women who established churches, revived dead churches, and stimulated lethargic churches. *The Baptist Basket* tells how young Agnes Wilson, a "girl bachelor" earning her own living in 1890 and "yet retaining all those pretty traits of a woman," inspired a dying church to come alive. [6] The same paper the next year told about a Georgia church about to disband, but "the women went to work and that stimulated the men," and the church revived. The pastor said, "that society was the means of saving our church." [7]

The growth of a multiple-staff ministry in Baptist churches is largely a twentieth-century development. A century ago the pastor was the only paid staff member, with possible exception of a janitor. Some large churches had assistant pastors in the eighteenth century, but this did not become common practice until toward the close of the nineteenth century. Some of the earliest nonpastoral church employees were women. They were called "Bible Women," or "Local Missionaries," and their work was mostly in church visitation, Sunday School canvassing, and counseling with women.[8] Women also had a considerable influence upon the development of Baptist worship practices, particularly in the area of music.

Women and Stewardship

In the area of stewardship Southern Baptist women have made one of their greatest contributions. To appreciate their work, one must see the stewardship heritage of Southern Baptists in historical perspective. The early Southern Baptist Convention was not particularly stewardship conscious. In 1873, 1884, and 1888 the SBC adopted major statements on stewardship, but none of them mentioned tithing. Most Southern Baptists had never heard of tithing, and those who had mostly opposed it because it sounded too much like the hated church tax that Baptists had been forced to pay in colonial days. Some Baptists could not even pronounce "tithe," making it rhyme with "Smith."

In 1884 the SBC spoke of the need for some systematic plan of Christian stewardship but admitted it could not come up with any acceptable plan.[9] Not until 1894 did the Convention clearly recommend the practice of tithing, and it was many years later before that teaching showed up consistently in SBC Sunday School curriculum materials.[10]

However, Southern Baptist women had taught and practiced tithing for years. Their publications, such as *The Heathen Helper* and *The Baptist Basket,* stressed the importance of regular, systematic giving. They clearly taught tithing several years before the denomination generally accepted it. There is every reason to believe the women influenced the churches and denomination in this matter.

The women also devised the plan whereby one's offering was placed in an envelope and its purpose marked. There is no record of Baptist churches using offering envelopes before they learned it from the WMU. Women also stressed the importance of regular giving each week, even if the amount was small. Instead of saving up one's offering until the amount became significant, they urged regular giving. This was quite contrary to earlier Baptist practice, where churches often had only one or two offerings a year. These were sometimes called the spring and fall "roundups." Some Baptist churches had only one offering a year, and it was largely by outside subscription rather than at church. Some Baptists who were willing to give would have been offended by an offering taken at church.

The women changed all this. They insisted that giving is more than a practical necessity; it is an act of worship and should be part of every Sunday's service. The extensive and effective stewardship program of Southern Baptists to this day owes much of its basic inspiration and methods to the women. The women also taught tithing to the children, and their magazines carried many articles on how to enlist husbands in giving. Over and over they emphasized that people do not give because they are not asked. "Let some sister in each church canvas the entire membership," they said.[11]

At Houston in 1925 the women launched a Convention-wide tithing program. They urged the use of tithing record cards, seal and pins, all forerunners of our church promotions and records of today. They also sponsored "Tithing Schools," and tithing story contests among young people, distributed books and tracts on tithing, and popularized the idea that only what is given beyond the tithe is an offering.

Women and Religious Education

The Sunday School, like other innovations, had a difficult time winning acceptance from Southern Baptists. However, there is reason to think that Baptist women saw the value of Sunday School before the men did. After all, they had always had the task of religious education of children and youth. Probably Marty is right that the early Sunday School was "often opposed by ministers not simply because it was new or was a threat to established ways of doing things but because it was often in the hands of women."[12] The paradoxical fact is that among Southern Baptists, a denomination that often forbade its women to teach in the church, Sunday School teaching was from the first, primarily a ministry of women.

Southern Baptist literature is replete with evidence of the leading role of women in the Sunday School. This was seen as an acceptable work for women, so long as they did not teach men or mixed classes. J. R. Graves of Tennessee in 1879 showed awareness that many Baptist women wanted to serve Christ but had few opportunities. He said, "Many seek a solution of this question in Sunday-school work."[13] As early as 1877 the SBC took official notice of the importance of women in Sunday School work.

During the years Southern Baptists had no Sunday School board, the women not only helped form and staff the schools, they also provided some of the literature. Baptist women in Baltimore formed a "Literature Department" in 1886 in connection with their missionary library and reading room.

Women circulated a wide variety of Bible study leaflets, usually with a missionary theme. They showed that there was a demand for such study helps, that their distribution could be not only feasible but actually profitable, and that they could be used to build Baptist loyalty and cooperation. Perhaps the example of the women in the literature ministry helped influence the SBC to form its own Sunday School Board in 1891.

Women also influenced Southern Baptist education. Some Baptists were among those who challenged the ancient idea that only boys should be educated. Some families, like the family of Lottie Moon in Virginia, provided equal education, as far as it was available, for their daughters.

Higher education was, along with missions, one of the dynamic forces around which scattered Baptist churches coalesced into a close-knit denomination in the early nineteenth century. A wave of Baptist colleges date from the 1830's and 1840's. Most Baptists, as others at that time, opposed coeducation, but they wanted schools for their daughters. The result was a wave of women's schools throughout the south. After 1880 a running debate raged in Baptist life, as in the nation, about the advantages of coeducation. Many of the women's colleges have survived to the present, but after the turn of the century more Baptist schools were open to both men and women.

Theological education of Southern Baptist women grew out of women in missions. As the Convention began to appoint single women as missionaries in the 1870's there was need for them to be informed on the Bible. Women missionaries rapidly learned the language of their mission field, but they often had little opportunity for serious Bible study.

By 1889 there were calls for a Baptist seminary for young women just as there was one for young men.[15] Had there been financial resources, no doubt a separate theological seminary for women would have been founded. Instead, a few women simply showed up on the campus of Southern Baptist Seminary in Louisville.

There is mention of one or two women sitting in seminary classes earlier than 1904, but in the autumn of that year there were four. Though not admissible as students, they won the advocacy of Eliza Broadus. Her father, seminary professor John A. Broadus, was an outspoken critic of women's speaking in church. Baptist women in the Louisville area raised money to rent a home for the young women adjacent to the campus. Soon the support was widened to include women throughout Kentucky. In 1907 this effort was organized into the Missionary Training School and adopted as a project of WMU. The school was able to purchase property with a gift of $20,000 from the Sunday School Board.

In 1906 there were 35 young women attending the seminary. They could attend class but could not raise questions or participate in class discussions. They did not take examinations. Upon completion of the courses, they did not receive a degree from the seminary but a certificate from the Training School.

One influential editor commended the work because it would be more economical than a separate school, guarantee the women orthodox training under the control of men, and provide a source of suitable wives for the men students. Above all, "Our Seminary will prevent the young women from becoming preachers, granting that any of them should so far miss their aim." [16]

Status of Women in the Convention

The question of women voting arose in the SBC just as it did in American society, and at about the same time. We have already seen that some, but not all, Baptist churches allowed women to vote on local church matters. However, the question of women's serving as delegates to association and convention meetings proved far more controversial.

Northern and Southern Baptist women had similar experiences on the question of official representation in the denomination. In 1876 one or two churches sent "female delegates" to the Trenton Association in New Jersey, where they were challenged. After a year of study the association voted to reject them out of fear that this would be the opening wedge by which women would demand "a right to vote, to debate all questions, to serve on Committees, to share in looking after derelict ministers and churches, to occupy the position of Clerk, or to sit in the Moderator's chair. Women will . . . demand perfect equality with male delegates." [17]

To avoid such calamity the majority brought a report to reject women delegates. However, the report was tabled and never removed. Northern Baptist women went quietly ahead and registered as delegates at the various associations and were soon accepted without question.

In Southern Baptist life women had been admitted as messengers in some of the state conventions by the end of the century, beginning with Kentucky in 1869. In North Carolina women could represent circles and societies but not churches. Before 1900 a few women in state conventions began to serve on committees, and even to address the state conventions. [18]

Representation became an issue at the Southern Baptist Convention of 1885, when two women were among the seven messengers from Arkansas. They were Mrs. J. P. Eagle, wife of the speaker of the Arkansas House of Representatives, and Mrs. M. D. Early, wife of a prominent pastor. Both women had been active for years in missionary activity in Arkansas and beyond. However, they were not crusaders and were both surprised and chagrined to see the commotion their appointment caused.

The husbands defended their wives valiantly. Early said he had at first objected to his wife's being named a messenger, but upon examination of the constitution could see no reason she should be ineligible. He concluded that "The question before this Convention is, Shall the Baptist ladies of this country, who have sent more money into the vaults of this Convention than the men, be excluded from a part in its deliberations?" [19]

Eagle, an attorney, wanted the women admitted as a right and not on the basis of some constitutional loophole. He said: "These ladies do a great work in Arkansas. They have done more, perhaps, in that State for missions than all the men. But if you think that the presence of these ladies will do any harm to the work of this Convention, then exclude them." [20]

Reverend O. C. Pope of Texas correctly pointed out that women had been enrolled as messengers previously. In 1877 and again in 1882, Myra E. Graves, widow of Baylor University president Henry

L. Graves, registered as a delegate without incident. She registered simply as "M. E. Graves," so perhaps the significance of her presence was overlooked. At any rate, if the "woman question" had not become so controversial, the custom of enrolling women as members of the Convention might have become fixed.

The Arkansas women were challenged by J. William Jones, elderly and conservative minister from Virginia, a state which was slow to approve organized work of Southern Baptist women. The SBC president appointed a five-man committee to consider the question. They included Jones of Virginia, Basil Manly of Kentucky, J. H. Kilpatrick of Georgia, L. L. Carroll of North Carolina, and M. B. Wharton of Alabama. Probably all five were opposed to admitting the women, but three of the five were "strict constructionists" who had to admit that the constitution did not exclude them. Manly spoke for the majority when he said, "If the constitution admits them, we must admit them." [21]

Older ministers clamored to be heard, saying that they were present at the 1845 formative meeting, and that if the constitution itself did not forbid women members it was only because at that time nobody could have anticipated such a foolhardy possibility. Two members of the committee brought a minority report to forbid the women to register. By a vote of 202 to 112 the Convention passed a motion to *substitute* the minority report for the majority report. However, the Convention never voted upon the report, for the women anticipated the outcome and withdrew their names. At that point, "a question was asked if this matter would appear in the minutes. The chair answered, *You have done nothing, and nothing will be recorded.*" [22]

This left the issue hanging. Three days later Jones brought up the question again and secured the appointment of a seven-man committee to bring another report. They recommended that the wording in Article III of the constitution on membership substitute the word "brethren" for the original reading of "messengers." This was adopted by a substantial majority. This restrictive wording remained in the constitution for thirty-three years.

Some feared that admitting women would lead to further representation. Jones said, "For forty years the Convention has been in existence, and never yet had a female taken part in its deliberation." [23]

He feared that if two ladies were seated the Convention "would be flooded with them next year." Another who opposed admitting the ladies said, "I love the ladies, but I dread them worse." Others feared the women might be "taking possession of the Convention, and occupying the president's chair." [24]

It is interesting that immediately before the final vote on exclusion, there was an offering for missions at which women made the most sacrificial contributions. Immediately after the exclusion, one brother "made a plea for the cooperation of the women" in mission support.

Although no woman made a speech, their response to exclusion was clear. They were more than a little resentful. Dr. Eaton of Kentucky, an opponent of the women, said: "he was requested by the ladies to say that while they did not care to speak, they did desire to hear. They who had been denied seats among the delegates, hoped they would speak loud enough for them to hear." [25]

For almost twenty years most of the women who attended SBC sessions at all, sat in the balcony.

It is a tribute to Southern Baptist women that they did not separate entirely from the Convention after the 1885 action. But with patience and perseverance, they continued to seek a workable form of cooperation.

A modern reader might well wonder why Baptists should become so exercised about women as Convention messengers, especially since they sat in several state conventions without tipping the world off its axis. It would be a misreading of history to regard this as merely a Baptist feud about the Convention. This was the voice of Southern Baptists against the entire feminist movement. Other opinions recorded from the 1885 convention show that Baptists were seriously concerned not to appear to endorse any part of the women's movement of the time.

Of course, some women approved the 1885 action. Mrs. James Hine of Georgia doubtlessly expressed the views of many women when she wrote that "most Christian women, those who are Bible readers and indoctrinated in the belief that women should be 'keepers at home,' and not be suffered to speak in the church, fully endorse this change." Since the SBC handles a great deal of money, the faithful men have a duty to "see that no heads inferior to their own . . . . be allowed to gather up the threads of this vast network of missions."

Even so, Mrs. Hine admitted that only two women among such male wisdom could have done little harm, but soon the "council halls might have been swarming with them, and with the impetuosity which belongs to their sex and the free use of the tongue with which they are gifted." Instead of seeking to be messengers to conventions, Hine suggested that women be content to "form mission bands among the sisterhood." [26]

From 1885 to 1918 women were excluded from membership in the Southern Baptist Convention. However, some probably attended the sessions, as evidenced by the 1913 provision, that women be "admitted to the floor upon their badges." As early as 1914 R. H. Coleman of Dallas indicated to the Convention his intention to move to change the constitution back to admit women. However, the matter proved so volatile that no action was taken until 1917. Over a thousand women registered at the WMU meeting in New Orleans in connection with the Convention that year. Observers reported that "applause from the women in the gallery greeted Dr. Coleman as he read his proposal" in 1917.[27] However, this resolution precipitated one of the most acrimonious debates and difficult parlimentary tangles of the Convention.

Coleman's resolution passed handily, but SBC president J. B. Gambrell ruled (probably erroneously) that any constitutional change requires a vote of two-thirds of those present and voting. It was the only time the constitution has been so interpreted. S. P. Brooks of Texas appealed from the ruling, but Gambrell's personal popularity was high, and the Convention sustained the chair. Once again women were denied a place in the Convention.

However, public response to the 1917 technicality was almost uniformly unfavorable. The *Baptist Standard* of Texas reported that: "The woman question is not settled; and we confidently expect, after a few years, when certain brethren will have learned the way of the Lord more perfectly, to see the elect sisters admitted to the Convention on the same basis as the men, just as we do in Texas." [28]

There seemed a general feeling that Baptists had delayed too long on this matter. When Coleman persistently reintroduced the resolution in 1918, he was prepared for another long debate. However, to the surprise of many, the Convention immediately passed the matter by an overwhelming vote, and moved with relief on to other matters.

Baptist reaction to the 1918 action was uniformly favorable. The influential editor of the *Religious Herald* said, "Thus we have given tardy recognition to the good women who are doing such noble work in carrying out all the tasks undertaken by Southern Baptists." [29] He urged that women be given representation on every Convention board, and asked: "Who can name a single valid reason why this should not be done? A dozen valid reasons why it should be done can be stated." [30]

Perhaps Lee Scarborough of Texas spoke for many when he said, "The Convention rightly recognized women as folks, sharing in the obligations and responsibilities of the Convention." He reminded that Baptists have long asked women for their time, labor, money, and "to give their sons to preach, and their daughters to be missionaries," and now they will also have a voice. [31]

Baptist Attitudes Toward Women

No doubt Spain is correct that "Southern Baptists opposed the organized feminist movement and all other efforts to effect any significant change in the traditional role of women in society." [32] A survey of Southern Baptist state papers, resolutions of conventions, and publications such as books and pamphlets bears out Spain's assessment. Southern Baptists spoke out often and almost with one voice against women's voting or speaking in mixed assemblies, women as preachers, and coeducation.

An 1868 article on "Female Education" rejected coeducation, which is based on "the erroneous opinion that the mental powers of the sexes are equal." The writer said that women's minds, like their bodies, have less strength than men, but this is compensated in that women's minds, like their bodies, have more beauty and symmetry than men's. [33]

A similar opinion was expressed in the *Religious Herald* of May 7, 1874. The writer denied that woman is man's intellectual or spiritual equal, on the basis that Eve could be deceived by the serpent, but Adam could not. He also denied that woman, whom he calls "man's chief ornament," is capable of producing any great literature, inventions, or legislation.

The widely influential Tennessee editor, J. R. Graves, said in 1879 that "woman has a place in the church," but spent most of the article to prove that that place is not the pulpit. He said, "Paul forbids woman to occupy the position of a public speaker or preacher, as being contrary to her womanly nature and at variance with the law of God." [34] This sums up the two prongs of Baptist opposition to leadership of women—her supposed delicate nature, and the law of God.

The idea of a woman's preaching, or even speaking at all to a mixed group, was the issue that most agitated Southern Baptist men. There was a flood of opposition to such practices in the literature of the late nineteenth century, and indeed to our own time.

A typical example is the editorial "Once for All," in the *Biblical Recorder* of February 10, 1892. The editor cited many new fads in the country, most of which start in the north and move south. "Among these is the determined effort to bring women to the front as public lecturers, or speakers before mixed assemblies, or as ordained preachers of the gospel." he said, "Once for all, let it be known *everywhere* that our people South, as a rule, are unalterably opposed to this thing." As for woman preachers, "We have a few pastors and laymen South, even in the Baptist churches," that favor this "unscriptural and dangerous innovation." He said Baptists "do not propose to be persuaded, cajoled, or drawn by the force of public or private opinion, into adopting this unscriptural and foolish practice." He called on Southern Baptist churches to refuse the use of their buildings to all woman speakers, no matter how good their cause.

This writer even objected to the growing Baptist Young People's Union (BYPU) on the ground that it allowed young girls to speak in assemblies attended by teenage boys. However, he did see value in the BYPU if it could be purged of this northern innovation of having both boys and girls on the program. He suggested that there be separate boys' and girls' groups, with boys doing all the public speaking even for the girls' groups.

Similar opinions were expressed by Tandy L. Dix, M.D., evidently a Southern Baptist layman, who wrote an article on "Sex" in 1886.

The doctor explained at length wherein women are biologically and psychologically inferior, and unfitted for "the machine shop, the halls of higher learning, and the legislative halls." He objected to coeducation because it would "bring ruin to domestic institutions and family relations, to the family altar, and hearthstone happiness; and the most important of all, ruin to a healthful procreation of our race."

The welfare of the human race, Dix insisted, depended upon "the maintenance and cultivation of effeminancy in the female." She must be restricted to the care of husband, children, the easel, the piano, and the needle. Dix objected to women's speaking in public, and he was especially incensed at the idea of women doctors. He claimed to put these views before the public in order "if possible to save some silly woman from the mortification she would suffer from placing herself before the public." [35]

That a major Southern Baptist paper would publish such views tells a great deal about Southern Baptist attitudes. Similar views could be quoted from virtually every Baptist paper of the time. Always the writers appealed to the Bible for support of their views that women should remain at home, that women should keep silent in the church, that woman was inferior because Eve was deceived rather than Adam. Southern Baptist men were not hesitant to place the blame for the fall of the race upon woman.

Occasionally there was a dissenting voice. Fred D. Hale of Owensboro, Kentucky, wrote in 1895 that given equal opportunity, boys and girls were equal in intellectual capacity. The denial of this he called "a heathen notion." He insisted that "She can think as profoundly, reason as logically, and put her thoughts into clear, vigorous and beautiful language as her supposed-to-be intellectual superior. Women can write as good books, articles or editorials, frame as good laws, render as just decisions, construct as good arguments, reach as wise conclusions, . . . and do everything else that requires a well-balanced and highly-cultured intellect as well as men in like circumstances can do." [36]

Though Hale says woman *can* do these things, he goes on to say she probably should not. Her God-given place is in the home, and she injures herself, her husband, and society if she tries to compete with men in the workaday world.

Some men helped women get a hearing. When missionary Mina Everett had to leave Brazil because of her health in 1888, the wife of a Brazilian pastor said with tears, "Oh Dona Mina! Plead in behalf of our country every time you have an opportunity." Miss Everett was grieved that she had no opportunity to plead in the churches. However, she was later employed by the women of Texas to travel the state speaking to women's groups. Once J. M. Carroll managed "by some careful persuasion" to allow her to speak to men and women at an associational meeting "at ten o'clock, it being the Sunday school and not the church hour." [37]

Probably most Southern Baptist women agreed generally with the assessment of men upon their "place" in society and church. There is no evidence that numbers of Southern Baptist women wanted to be preachers. However, some women resented the superiority complex of the men who discussed the subject. Mary T. Gambrell of Meridian, Mississippi, wrote an interesting rejoinder to a sermon by William T. Harvey, published in the *Western Recorder.* Harvey was one of the most militant Baptist spokesmen against women's speaking in public. In *The Baptist Basket,* a magazine published by women, Gambrell scoffed at Harvey's "guarding the pulpit against the sacrilegious tread of feminine feet." She assures her readers that "we did not share in the Dr.'s dread lest the activity of women in Missions presaged a violation of Scripture precedent and precept." [38]

Another writer in the same issue commented with approval on the practice of some women in Indian Territory who kept their birthright name after marriage, had freedom to choose their own husbands and divorce them if they proved lazy or tyrannical, and who had to be consulted on family business decisions. Clearly the women liked these ideas, which were described as "a thunderbolt of solid information." [39]

After the turn of the century, Baptist attitudes toward women began to moderate. This can be seen from a major 1915 editorial in the *Baptist Courier* which responded to requests from women readers to discuss the issue. The editor acknowledged the vast changes in society, and implied that these could affect interpretation of the Pauline passages. We also said there is no clear division of men/women church roles in the Bible. He continued, "This is one of the issues on which Baptists have long been somewhat divided. . . .

How far ought our women to go? Can they give their testimony at prayer meeting? Can they be presented at associations and conventions and when presented can they utter a few words? Must they speak at all when men are present?" [40]

At least some progress is evident in that these questions were left open. In fact, the editor suggested that such questions be left to the women to decide for themselves.

Summary

The nineteenth century was important for women in America, including Baptists. During these years they sought and found their place in Southern Baptist life. Women made great contributions, not only in missions, but also in stewardship, education, Sunday Schools, and local church ministries.

Opposition to the emerging roles of women was severe during these years. Not only did women have to cope with a barrage of editorials, sermons, and books seeking to keep them in their "place," they also were disenfranchised from the Southern Baptist Convention.

However, by the end of the century Baptist women had made some progress. We now turn our attention to the twentieth century.

Notes

[1] Leon McBeth, *The First Baptist Church of Dallas 1868-1968* (Grand Rapids: Zondervan Publishing House, 1968), 25f.

[2] *Baptist Courier,* May 14, 1885, 2.

[3] *Confederate Baptist,* December 14, 1864, 2.

[4] Ibid.

[5] Lynn E. May, Jr. *The First Baptist Church of Nashville, Tennessee, 1820-1970* (Nashville: First Baptist Church, 1970), 106.

[6] *Baptist Basket,* October, 1891, 80-81.

[7] Ibid., 136.   [8] Ibid., 66, 86.

[9] *SBC Annual,* 1884, 20.

[10] *SBC Annual,* 1894, 26.

[11] *Baptist Basket,* October 1891, 136.

[12] Martin E. Marty, *The Pro and Con Book of Religious America* (Waco, Texas: Word Books, 1975), Con, 98.

[13] *The Baptist,* February 22, 1879.

[14] *SBC Annual,* 1877, 20.

[15] Ethlene Boone Cox, *Following in His Train* (Nashville: Broadman Press, 1938), 178.

[16] *Biblical Recorder,* March 14, 1906.

[17] Norman H. Maring, *Baptists in New Jersey* (Valley Forge: Judson Press, 1964), 233.

[18] Rufus B. Spain, *At Ease in Zion: A Social History of Southern Baptists, 1865-1900* (Nashville: Vanderbilt University Press, 1967), 169-70.

[19] *Alabama Baptist,* May 14, 1885, 2.

[20] Ibid.   [21] Ibid.   [22] Ibid.

[23] *Tennessee Baptist,* May 14, 1885, 6.

[24] *Tennessee Baptist,* May 30, 1885, 6.

[25] *Tennessee Baptist,* May 23, 1885, 6.

[26] *Christian Index,* July 2, 1885, 3.

[27] *Baptist and Reflector,* May 24, 1917.

[28] *Baptist Standard,* May 24, 1917, 6.

[29] *Religious Herald,* May 23, 1918, 4.

[30] Ibid.

[31] *Baptist Standard,* May 30, 1918.

[32] Spain, 165.

[33] *Biblical Recorder,* August 26, 1868.

[34] *The Baptist,* February 22, 1879.

[35] *Western Recorder,* January 7, 1886, 2.

[36] *Religious Herald,* February 7, 1895.

[37] J. M. Carroll, *A History of Texas Baptists* (Dallas: Baptist Standard Publishing Company, 1923), 861.

[38] *Baptist Basket,* October 1891, 138.

[39] Ibid., 147.

[40] August 20, 1915, 4.

SIX

Women Taking Their Place

Twentieth Century Southern Baptist Women

Municipal Auditorium buzzed with excitement that Saturday morning in Memphis as the Southern Baptist Convention prepared to hear the annual report of the Woman's Missionary Union. This might have been routine, for there had been forty such annual reports since 1888. However, 1929 was different. This year a *woman* would give the WMU report!

As Mrs. W. J. Cox rose to speak to the packed house, she must have been keenly aware of the historical significance of the occasion. For years after its formation in 1888 the WMU made its report through the Foreign Mission Board. Even after it began to report directly to the Convention in 1913, the reports were always given by a man. While this was not the first time a woman had spoken before the Convention, Cox gave the first major address by a woman. This was also the first time the WMU president made her annual report in person directly to the Convention.

Mrs. Cox must have known of concerted efforts to prevent her from speaking. The Convention issued the invitation in 1928, with no recorded opposition, but during the year controversy flared. The issue of a woman addressing a mixed assembly was debated in several Baptist state papers and in various meetings of pastors. The General Association of Baptists in Kentucky, led by J. W. Porter, passed a resolution against the idea, claiming that to allow a woman to speak in a mixed assembly would go against the Bible and 1900 years of historical precedent.

As time drew near for Cox to speak, Porter introduced the following resolution:

Whereas, the Convention has invited the president of the W.M.U. to address this session of the body; therefore, be it

Resolved, That while expressing our appreciation of the president of the W.M.U., we earnestly protest the president of the W.M.U. or any other woman addressing this Convention;

Resolved, That it is the sense of this body that it is unscriptural for a woman to address this body.[1]

An observer noted that: "The resolution was sent at once without debate to the Resolutions Committee, where it will sleep indefinitely, of course." [2] His prophecy proved correct, but even after this setback, several die-hard opponents continued to seek ways to prevent Mrs. Cox from speaking. As several clamored for recognition from the floor, the stately Convention president, George W. Truett, stepped to the podium. His powerful personality and white-haired dignity quieted the auditorium, and he said, "Brethren, let us hear the gentlewoman." Even as Cox rose to speak, a well-known brother picked up his hat and walked out with the comment he would not remain to hear a woman violate Scripture.

Mrs. Cox gave her message, which was well-received by the Convention. This was a significant breakthrough in the role of women in the SBC, a fact not lost upon Cox. In response to efforts to bar her from the program, she said, "No woman went to sleep in the garden. No woman denied Him. No woman betrayed Him. But it was a woman, acting in intuition, who tried to save Him."

Not until 1938, however, did women regularly give the WMU report. In that fiftieth anniversary year Mrs. Cox again gave the report, and Mrs. F. W. Armstrong addressed the Convention.

Baptist Women in New Roles

Can you imagine a woman from 1878 attending the 1978 SBC in Atlanta? Such a visitor from the past might well have been overwhelmed. She would know nothing of airplanes and automobiles, and such a *large* convention as Atlanta would have been unthinkable a century ago. She might have been delighted with air conditioning in the hotels (if not in the convention hall itself). She would of course notice at once that the bonnets and hoop skirts of the earlier era had given way to more casual styles.

But our visitor might be most astonished by the *women* at the Atlanta convention. First, they were *there,* thousands of them.

Women were official messengers, the same as men, and voted on issues and elections just as did the men. A woman was the featured speaker at the gigantic Pastors Conference, and a woman was nominated for the vice-presidency of the Convention.

More than that, at one point the Convention was asked to express its opinion on the subject of ordaining women to the ministry. There is no way the women of 1878, or the men either, could have anticipated such far-reaching changes in the status and role of women in one century. This section will trace briefly some of these changes and how they took place.

We have seen in a previous chapter how women obtained status as official messengers to the SBC in 1918. The fact that women were granted the franchise in the United States by the nineteenth amendment only two years later, shows the close connection between changing roles of women in society and church. After 1918 the record shows that women took advantage of their new status, and attended the Convention as messengers in good numbers. A count of registrants to the 1919 SBC showed that 109 women registered from Alabama alone, out of a total of 475 messengers from that state. The same year, 30 of 127 messengers from Arkansas were women.[3]

However, women did not move immediately into places of leadership. One or two women served on Convention boards in the 1920's, but from 1927 to 1958 only five women served on the influential Executive Committee. No dramatic changes in the voting patterns in the Convention can be attributed to the new votes by women. By the 1978 SBC in Atlanta men composed 55.9 percent of messengers, women 42.1 percent, with 2 percent not indicating. This was up slightly from the previous year, when 40.2 percent of registered messengers were women.

One careful researcher says that: "From 1929 to 1966 there were no significant Convention actions relative to women and their involvement in the Convention." [4] Nevertheless, during these years women gradually moved into at least limited representation on some committees at state and national levels. In 1961 various SBC committees had 800 members, of whom 20 were women. By 1971 this had risen to 42 of a total of 927.[5] In six years the percentage of women on boards and commissions of the SBC has risen from 4.7 percent in 1972 to 8.6 percent in 1977, with continued increases since then.

The most dramatic increase has come since 1974 when the Christian Life Commission recommended a change in Convention bylaws to require that at least 20 percent of all agency boards and commissions be composed of women. Though the Convention rejected this motion, it did serve to call dramatic attention to the underrepresentation of women at decision-making levels.

At the time of the 1974 Convention only one agency, the Home Mission Board, was near the recommended 20 percent level. However, in 1977 women constituted more than 20 percent of the boards of four agencies, including the Historical Commission (23.5 percent); the Christian Life Commission (23.3 percent); the Home Mission Board (20.2 percent); and the Foreign Mission Board (20.2 percent).[6]

However, in 1977 women made up only five of the 65 members of the powerful Executive Committee (7.7 percent), and four of the 84 trustees of the Sunday School Board (4.8 percent). In 1977 the Southern Baptist Theological Seminary in Louisville had 4 women among its 61 trustees, while the other five seminaries each had one woman on their boards. The Education Commission had one woman on its board, while the Radio and Television Commission had none.

As to employment, in 1961 the Baptist Sunday School Board had women in only 2.5 percent of its managerial posts, a figure that had risen to 6.7 percent by 1971.[7]

The men who voted to exclude women as messengers to the Convention might have been amazed that scarcely less than a century later women would serve as officers of the Convention. In 1963 Mrs. R. L. Mathis was elected a vice-president of the Convention, the first woman to be chosen for such a post. Mrs. J. M. Dawson was nominated in 1923 but failed of election.[8] Mathis was elected on Thursday, and on Friday a messenger from Kansas moved to amend the Constitution by limiting officers to the male sex. His motion was ruled out of order and the election of Mathis stood.[9]

In 1975 bitter debate about the proper role of women in religion probably contributed to the defeat of another woman nominated for vice-president. However, in 1976 Mrs. Carl E. Bates of North Carolina was elected to that office. In 1978 the popular singer-entertainer Anita Bryant was defeated by more than 2 to 1 for the vice-presidency. Bryant spoke to a packed house at the Pastors Conference, and most observers felt her election was a certainty should she be nominated. However, she had become quite controversial as an outspoken opponent of homosexual groups in the country. It would be difficult to assess whether her defeat was due to Baptist unwillingness to be identified with her moral crusade, her admittedly scant credentials for the office, or the fact she was a woman. As of 1978, no woman had been elected or even nominated as Convention president.

Reactions to New Roles

These new leadership roles for women have not been without opposition in Southern Baptist life. There have been sharp reactions and resistance by many men and even a few women. Some of this has been a carryover from the almost universal Baptist opposition to the women's liberation movement of the nineteenth century, and general if not unanimous opposition to a similar movement in the present century. Some of the opposition arises out of honest differences in interpreting Scripture, since some men (and women) believe the Bible forever forbids women from meaningful leadership roles.

The move to grant the franchise to Southern Baptist women in 1918 by allowing them to be Convention messengers took years to accomplish. For a few years after 1885 it was not clear whether women were even welcome at Convention sessions as silent spectators. At times women were relegated to balconies, though after 1900 members of the WMU could be "admitted to the floor on their badges," i.e. their credentials as members of WMU.

However, sentiment was growing in the nation and in the SBC, to allow a larger role for women. As early as 1914 R. H. Coleman of Dallas announced his intention to change the constitution to allow women to be messengers. But despite the persistent and well-planned efforts of Coleman and several other leaders of influence, they were not able to accomplish this change until 1918. Convention messengers voted it down, stalled, resorted to technicalities to prevent its consideration, and in one case even when a clear majority voted to admit women, the president ruled the vote invalid on a technicality.

Dire predictions by ultraconservatives followed the 1918 vote. Led by J. W. Porter of Kentucky, who would ten years later oppose Mrs. Cox's speaking to the Convention, many feared this action would encourage more women to attend the Convention, encourage them to speak out in Convention discussions, serve on committees, speak in mixed audiences, or even someday serve as Convention officers!

Perhaps the best example of this opposition was J. W. Porter's publication in 1923 of *Feminism: Woman and Her Work*.[10] Edited and with a major chapter by Porter, this book picked up and reprinted articles by leading Southern Baptist opponents of women in leadership roles from years past. Sample chapters include such as: "Should a Woman Speak in Mixed Assemblies?" by John A. Broadus; "Women Speaking in Mixed Assemblies," by J. B. Hawthorne; "The Bible on Women's Public Speaking," by T. T. Eaton; "Shall Women Preach?" by W. P. Harvey; and "Commentary on Corinthians and Timothy," by B. H. Carroll. Most of these were written originally in the nineteenth century, but were reprinted by Porter.

Porter's own chapter, "The Menace of Feminism," is one of the most critical in the book. Porter said: "In 1918 the Southern Baptist Convention, meeting at Hot Springs, Arkansas, by a formal vote opened the way for women to become messengers to that body. It was then understood and has since transpired that this would be followed by women membership on boards, women speakers before mixed assemblies, etc. It was probably not generally understood that this action inevitably slants in the direction of women preachers, but such is now believed to be the case by many Baptists, who point to this unscriptural practice as an actual consummation among not a few American evangelical bodies." [11]

To stanch the flow in this direction, Porter put out this book which received widespread attention from Southern Baptists. Porter complained that: "The Southern Baptist Convention has admitted women as messengers, and given them representation on committees—and the end is not yet. It goes without saying, that membership in a body of this character, carries with it all the rights and privileges of the body. What next? Would it not be entirely in order to appoint a woman as chairman of a committee, and permit her to speak to her report? May the time not come, when a woman shall preside over the Convention, and another preach the introductory sermon? It was freely predicted when women were admitted as messengers that, they would claim no further rights in this regard. But time has clearly demonstrated that this was the 'opening wedge' and it is now evident that even some of our Southern feminists are prepared to go the logical limit of their contention. At the recent meeting of the S.B.C. a woman came very near being elected Vice-President of the Convention." [12]

Porter expressed all the major arguments against any leadership role by women. He quoted from the Bible, physicians, educators, and clergymen to show that women are inferior in mind (though not in morals), and that for women to exercise any leadership in church would damage the health, homes, and happiness of all Americans. He seemed particularly upset by the "flapper" of his day, whom he saw as going out in public with "low-cut waist, high-cut skirt, corsetless, and perhaps, petticoatless." [13]

Gradually this opposition began to wane, though as late as 1962 a Southern Baptist pastor in Kentucky wrote an introduction for yet another reprint of the pamphlet by Broadus against women's speaking in mixed groups. The pastor said he felt such speaking was "in direct violation of clear and unmistakable commands of God," and he hoped his reprint would help to "ward off . . . liberalism." [14]

In more recent years opposition to women in leadership roles has come from the more fundamentalist groups. While many Southern Baptists today doubt that women should be ordained as ministers or even as deacons, probably very few would deny them representation on Convention committees.

The Twentieth-Century WMU

Baptist women through the WMU have become a major force in SBC life in this century. From the local church to the Convention itself the WMU and its related organizations have helped shape the attitudes and actions of Southern Baptists. The WMU and its leaders have been in the forefront of every major Convention program from the Seventy-five Million Campaign in 1919 to the Bold Mission Thrust in 1978. Through their mission structures, women have helped set the agenda for the denomination, and by their leadership, inspiration, and effective funding, have helped bring it to pass.

However, recent years have seen far-reaching changes in WMU and its related organizations. Like the churches and the Convention, this historic organization has been not static but vital and changing.

In this section we will set out some accomplishments of WMU, some ways it has changed, and seek to account for those changes.

Related organizations.—Early in this century the WMU developed a full program of missionary training for all age groups. After formation of Young Woman's Auxiliary in 1907, girls over 16 had their own mission group, as did children under 12 in the Sunbeam Band, a group formed earlier and adopted by WMU in 1890. In 1908, referring to boys and girls between 12 and 16 as "the mission link" WMU formed a new group. At first called Junior Young Women, the name Girl's Auxiliary was chosen in 1914, and was used until 1970 when this group became known as Acteens. Royal Ambassadors, a mission group for boys, was sponsored by WMU in 1908. In 1953 the Royal Ambassadors were transferred to sponsorship of the Men's Brotherhood. All of these organizations engaged in mission study and giving and helped promote missionary and stewardship consciousness among Southern Baptists.

The obvious success of the women's movement was probably a major factor in the organization of Baptist men in 1907 under the name of the Laymen's Mission Movement. This group has undergone a number of name changes, being known as the Baptist Brotherhood and now simply as Baptist Men. The men's group never had the impact of WMU either at local or Convention level. Perhaps one reason is that Baptist men were actively involved in the total church and had less need in the early days of a separate organization. Already the men were serving as pastors, deacons, committee chairmen. They were in places of leadership and active participation often not available to women. For the women the WMU provided the only place they could lead, speak out, and exercise their own leadership skills. Therefore, at least up to recent times, the WMU was far more important to women than the Brotherhood was to men.

The Margaret Fund.—A significant accomplishment of WMU is provision of scholarships for sons and daughters of missionaries through the Margaret Fund. Established in 1904 by an initial gift of $10,000 by Mrs. Frank Chambers, the fund was named in honor of her grandmother, mother, and daughter. This fund was used to purchase a house in Greenville, South Carolina, known as Margaret Home. It was to be used as a home for missionary children while at school in this country and also as a haven for furloughing missionaries. However, this arrangement largely restricted missionary youth to the local Baptist college in Greenville, so the home was sold in 1914 and the resulting Margaret Fund was used to award scholarships to young people to attend schools of their choice.

At first a typical scholarship was $300 a year, but this later rose to $500 and later to $1000. From 1916 to 1956, 777 students received Margaret Fund scholarship aid, to the amount of $857,279.43.[15] In 1961 the administration of Margaret Fund scholarships was transferred to the two mission boards, though WMU continues to award special scholarships from interest on trust funds.

Missionary Training School.—As early as 1872 the SBC was appointing single women missionaries, and even before that the wives of missionaries served alongside their husbands. While women could attend most Baptist colleges, they were not admitted to the one theological seminary sponsored by the denomination. This meant that Baptist women, including missionary appointees, were without any formal theological and biblical training.

This need came to the attention of the faculty of the Southern Baptist Theological Seminary in Louisville. A trustee committee reported in 1902:

> 1. That we find that there is a necessity, distinct and urgent for such a school for Southern Baptist women. . . .
> 2. That after conference with the Faculty of the Seminary we find that instruction well suited to the young women can be provided without expense to the Seminary.
> 3. That there are no dormitories or boarding arrangements for the young women at the Seminary. . . . We may hope that a suitable dormitory may be provided for the young women. . . .
> 4. That we commit this matter to the Faculty of the Seminary, requesting that the matter be duly considered, that they undertake such work in this direction as seems wise to them.[16]

While a step in the right direction, the provisions which came out of this action were inadequate. Young women were admitted to Seminary classes, but they were not required to perform the study assignments or write examinations, nor were they eligible for degrees. Moreover, the Seminary was not quite prepared for the influx of single young women seeking training. In 1904 four young women showed up to enroll, but in 1905 there were about thirty-five.

Eliza S. Broadus, whose father was a professor at the Seminary, called a meeting of Baptist women in Louisville to ask them to sponsor a home for the women students. What began as a local WMU project in Louisville grew until it was taken over by the Convention-wide WMU, much to the objection of Annie Armstrong. With the original Louisville property and with a grant from the Sunday School Board, the WMU erected a large dormitory for the women students.

This school was controlled entirely by WMU until 1956, when the SBC began to elect the trustees. In 1962 the school, then known as the Carver School of Missions and Social Work, was merged back with the Seminary, thus continuing the original trend. The Training School served a vital function in theological education for Baptist women in the days before seminaries were thoroughly open to them.

Originating at a later date when attitudes had already changed somewhat, the Southwestern Baptist Theological Seminary in Fort Worth never formed a separate department for women. In 1914 the wife of a ministerial student applied for enrollment in courses leading to a degree in theology. Reference to the seminary charter confirmed that the school had authority "to confer upon any pupil of said Seminary—or upon any other person any of the degrees usually conferred by theological seminaries, or other degrees arising from its curriculum." [17]

Upon the basis of the charter, seminary officials agreed that men and women were equally admissible to every degree program then and for the future, including all the doctoral programs. A number of women have received the doctorate of theology from Southwestern, beginning in the 1920's when this was quite unusual in Southern Baptist schools.

The Seventy-five Million Campaign.—In 1919 the SBC launched what was perhaps the most important special campaign in its history. Known as the $75 Million Campaign, this was an effort to raise that amount for all SBC causes over a five year period, 1919–24.

The times seemed right for such a drive. America had just successfully concluded World War I, and the country was prosperous and optimistic. The huge bond drives of the war years showed that Americans were willing to pledge and give vast amounts of money for causes dear to them. Other denominations were mounting similar drives, and every SBC agency seemed ready to launch a major expansion drive on its own. Instead of each agency's doing its own campaign, the SBC voted to combine all these into one gigantic drive.

The women's group supported the campaign with great enthusiasm, and participated in every phase of planning, promotion, and implementation. The entire campaign pledged over $92 million, but economic reversals cut actual receipts down to $58 million. The WMU pledged $15 million of this amount and actually went beyond the pledge by giving over $16 million.

With optimistic expectations, SBC agencies expanded rapidly in the early 1920s, mostly on borrowed money. When the expected $92 million did not come in, nor even the planned $75 million, Convention agencies, including the two mission boards, were deeply in debt and unable to pay. To add to Convention burdens, officials uncovered an embezzlement in the Home Mission Board of almost a million dollars.

In the depths of the depression, the SBC struggled to pay off its staggering load of debt. At first the WMU voted to concentrate its efforts on helping pay off debts of the Foreign Mission Board alone, but Louie D. Newton of Georgia made an impassioned plea that the women distribute their efforts toward the entire SBC debt, which they did. Women also participated in the "Hundred Thousand Club," an effort to enlist 100,000 Southern Baptists who would give $1 a month over and above other offerings to help defray debt. With a slogan of "debt free by '43," the SBC paid off its last debts in 1943.

Despite the burden of debt and too-rapid expansion, the $75 Million Campaign cannot be considered a failure. Out of this came a greater stewardship awareness. To conserve the good results, the Convention formed in 1925 the Cooperative Program. The WMU has been loyal in its support of the Cooperative Program, insisting only on its continued right to sponsor special offerings for foreign, home, and state missions.

Special anniversaries have marked WMU milestones. The Silver Anniversary in 1913 saw WMU more firmly integrated into the denomination. At the Ruby Anniversary in 1928 the WMU called for, and largely achieved, a 40 percent across-the-board growth in enrollment and gifts. The Diamond Anniversary in 1963 was celebrated with drama and pageantry and with renewed commitment to the Baptist Jubilee Advance program.

Several factors led women to headquarter the early WMU in Baltimore. Mrs. Graves had been there, as had Annie Armstrong, and Baltimore was an early center of women's mission interest. However, a desire for a more central location led to a move of headquarters to Birmingham in 1921.

In 1906 Annie Armstrong resigned as Corresponding Secretary after 18 effective and sometimes controversial years at the helm of WMU. She was succeeded by Edith Campbell Crane, who served until 1912. Others who have served as Corresponding Secretary include Kathleen Mallory, 1912-1948; Alma Hunt, 1948-1975; and Carolyn Weatherford, since 1975.

Like most organizations in American society, the WMU has changed and still is changing. However, amid the changes some fundamental things are the same. If Annie Armstrong might not recognize all the structures, programs, and printed materials of the modern WMU, she would certainly be right at home with the central missionary thrust, the utmost denominational loyalty, and the continuing effort to enlist women and children, and indeed all Baptists, in missionary study and giving.

Some recent changes in WMU include a reorganized structure, different kinds of programs and printed materials, and changes in the traditional missionary societies and circles. At times the membership has declined somewhat from the peak years. Organizations for girls and young women, while holding to the same basic purposes, have changed their names and approaches somewhat. At the national level the WMU is ever more firmly integrated as an agency of the SBC. What began in 1888 as an "auxiliary" with a tenuous and rather vague relation to the Convention is now just as much an integral part of the SBC as any other agency, though it still retains the name of auxiliary and reports under the heading of "Associated Organizations." The WMU is represented at the SBC Executive Committee and in the Interagency Council.

Many reasons might be advanced for changes within the WMU, as indeed within the churches themselves. Probably the WMU has been most affected by changes in society, particularly the increasing employment of women outside the home. This had radically reduced discretionary time for millions of women, and has made the traditional weekday WMU meeting almost a relic of the past. Some groups met at night, which led for awhile to the awkward distinction between Baptist "day women" (homemakers) and "night women" (employed outside).

The very success of WMU may also, paradoxically, have brought problems. Due largely to WMU efforts, the entire church has become involved in mission study and giving; the special foreign and home offerings are church-wide events in which men as well as women are involved. The fact that WMU's task has been assumed by the entire church means that it has succeeded, but its own sphere is thereby no longer quite so unique.

Women have become in recent years more active in the church itself. They teach, serve on and sometimes chair committees, make motions and speak on issues in church conference, serve on church staffs, and in some SBC churches serve as deacons or even as ordained ministers. In short, the entire church is now their sphere of activity, whereas in years past any woman who aspired to leadership usually found her place in WMU. Therefore women are no longer restricted to WMU, and perhaps some have found their service elsewhere.

The women's liberation movement has had a profound impact, especially on younger women. With raised consciousness and higher expectations, some young Baptist women who might have been recruits for WMU found the programs and activities too restricted for their newly liberated outlook. However, WMU has a history of adapting to changing times and has certainly done so in this case. Without altering its historic commitment to missions, and without projecting an image of militance, the WMU has adapted to welcome the more socially aware Southern Baptist woman and offer programs and activities to meet her needs. Even among Baptist women most outspoken for women's rights, there is high appreciation for WMU as the first Baptist agency to allow leadership for women.

Is there a new Southern Baptist woman? Probably the answer is yes, and the WMU is making every opportunity to offer viable channels of ministry for her.

The Convention and Women

The role of women in Baptist life arose as a controversial issue at the Portland convention in 1973 and has been a thorny issue at every convention since. At Portland, Mrs. Jesse Sappington, wife of a Houston pastor, presented a substitute for the resolution reaffirming the traditional roles of women in church and society and criticizing the modern women's liberation movement. Her resolution read in part:

> WHEREAS, The Scriptures bear record to the distinctive roles of men and women in the church and in the home, and
>
> WHEREAS, Christian women have made and are making a significant contribution to the cause of Christ, and
>
> . . . .
>
> WHEREAS, There is a great attack by members of most women's liberation movements upon scriptural precepts of woman's place in society
>
> . . . .
>
> Therefore, be it *Resolved,* that we "redig" or reaffirm God's order of authority for his church and the Christian home: (1) Christ the head of every man; (2) man the head of the woman; (3) children in subjection to their parents—in the Lord.[18]

However, the statement later reported back by the Resolutions Committee called on the convention to "give full recognition to women in leadership roles in church and denominational life." It bore little resemblance to the original resolution, with both wording and basic thrust changed, most observers thought. Sappington moved the original resolution be adopted, which, after discussion, was done.

A considerable uproar greeted this Convention action. Women protested that they had been disenfranchised, declared second-class citizens, and restricted to the arbitrary authority of men. Amid the furor few noticed that at the annual Ministers' Wives Luncheon in Portland, a leading Bible scholar told the wives, "The New Testament says you are free; the walls are down; the veil of the temple is open, so make your own contribution. . . . Women became the core of the first churches. They became deacons, they prayed, they prophesied, they led in worship." [19]

Increasing agitation on both sides guaranteed this issue would come up again in 1974, as indeed it did. In fact, the role of women dominated the Dallas convention in 1974, turning what might otherwise have been rather tame sessions into exciting confrontations. The Dallas convention took three actions relative to women, all controversial.

The Convention tabled (and thus killed) the first part of a Christian Life Commission report on "Freedom for Women." The statement said in part:

"The Bible champions human liberation. Paul, in reflecting upon the new life in Christ, wrote to the Galatians, "There is neither Jew nor Greek, there is neither slave nor free, there is neither male nor female; for you are all one in Christ Jesus" (Gal. 3:28).

"Both men and women share the freedom which Christ gives. Historically, men have enjoyed far more freedom than women. Yet, men are not as free as God means them to be, for when men keep women from being free, then both remain enslaved; and the work of Jesus Christ at this important point is made of no effect.

"Injustice toward women persists to some degree in every institution in society: government, business, education, and the church. So imbedded is discrimination against women that it affects not only the hearts and minds of people in society but also the institutions and structures of society itself. Unequal pay for the same kind of work is an example of the injustices against women which ought to be intolerable to Christians. Even in our churches, women often have been kept from assuming places of leadership for which their abilities and their Christian commitment qualify them.

"Just as it is sinful for men to discriminate against women, so it is sinful for women to refuse to accept the dignity God has bestowed upon them." [20]

Many messengers felt, correctly or not, this was a thinly veiled push for the ordination of women, and by overwhelming vote they tabled it.

Specific recommendations from the Christian Life Commission included the controversial paragraph four, reading:

(4) We recommend that the Southern Baptist Convention's Constitution and Bylaws, paragraph 5 [which is printed on pages

33-34 of the 1973 *Annual* of the Southern Baptist Convention as follows: "All Convention committees, boards and commissions shall include both ordained and lay persons as members. Not more than two-thirds of the members of any group should be drawn from either category."] of Bylaw 7 entitled "How Board Members, Trustees, Commissioners, or Members of Standing Committees Are Elected," be amended by adding as a move toward more equitable representation the following concluding sentence: *At least one-fifth of the total members shall be women.* [Since this recommendation involves a Bylaw change, it is understood that it requires a two-thirds vote of the Convention.] [21]

The chairman of the Commission pointed out that about 55 percent of SBC church members are women, but only about five percent of SBC board members are women. However, the messengers decisively voted down the proposed quota system. Despite this rejection, it is interesting to note the rapidly rising percentage of women elected to SBC boards.

By 1974 it was common knowledge that several women had been ordained as Southern Baptist deacons and ministers; in fact, some of them entered into debate at the Convention. Some thought the fact that the Home Mission Board had endorsed a woman for appointment as a chaplain implied SBC approval of her ordination.

A Texas messenger introduced a motion that the following be added to Article IX of the Constitution under the "Missionary Qualifications": "All appointments, endorsements, etc., (including the military and industrial chaplaincy) whose function will be that of a pastor, which is restricted to males by Scripture, must meet those requirements as outlined in the New Testament." [22]

This proposal was widely understood not only as a restriction upon chaplaincy endorsements by SBC agencies but as official Convention disapproval of the ordination of women. This proposal had considerable support in the Convention but failed of the two-thirds vote required for a change in the constitution. Its defeat left the question of ordination with the local church.

The generally quiet 1975 convention in Miami took some actions which relate, directly or indirectly, to the role of women. One messenger "made a motion to instruct the president to call a meeting of men now serving as presidents of the various state conventions to prepare and present to the 1976 Convention a statement of information and guidelines for the various agencies of the Convention to supplement the current 'Baptist Faith and Message Statement.' " [23] Some proponents of this motion apparently hoped such an addendum to the 1963 Confession would either forbid the ordination of women or forbid Convention agencies to recognize or endorse ordained women. However, the Convention refused to tamper with its Confession of Faith, and this motion was lost.

Meanwhile, at the Miami meeting of Ministers' Wives, W. A. Criswell of Dallas, speaking on the role of women in the church, said biblical statements about women must be interpreted in context. "Anytime a Baptist church wants to have deaconesses, it is perfectly Biblical," Criswell was reported to have said. "We don't do it because of tradition." [24] At the same convention Christine Gregory of Virginia, newly-elected president of WMU, took the position that women should be free to respond to God's call, whatever that call might involve. While eschewing ordination for herself, the wife of a Virginia layman said, "God created every individual with the right of choice. . . . If a woman feels she is called to be a pastor, this is between her and God, and it should not be our prerogative to deny her." [25]

While dominated by other issues (abortion and homosexuality, among others) the conventions of 1976 in Norfolk and 1977 in Kansas City made their contributions to the women's movement. This was not so much in formal votes, as by example. Newly elected SBC president Jimmy Allen of Texas, in a news conference endorsed equal rights for women, and urged Southern Baptists to open more doors to service opportunities for women in local Baptist churches. Citing the matter of ordaining women as a decision for the local churches rather than the Convention, Allen said, "I'm not as excited in the ordination of women as in freeing them for useful service. The question is, 'Are they allowed to be decision makers?' " [26]

At the same meeting Marian Grant of North Carolina was elected to chair a powerful Convention Committee on Order of Business. So far as is known, she was the first woman to chair a major SBC board or committee. Mrs. Grant, whose husband, J. Marse Grant, was editor of the state Baptist paper of North Carolina, also is an ordained deacon and has chaired the board of deacons in her church.

Once again, the Convention in Atlanta in 1978 faced the role of women, though it was by no means a major issue. Mrs. Sappington, who had become something of a Convention regular on this issue, presented a resolution calling for a vote by messengers on whether they favored the ordination of women. The Convention refused to be drawn into this controversial and potentially divisive issue and tabled the proposal. Messengers seemed to show more tolerance for women in church leadership positions, and neither those who favor ordination nor those who oppose it seemed to desire a confrontation. The Convention sought to turn its total energies to its program of Bold Mission Thrust and would brook no distractions.

A review of this data emphasizes that the Southern Baptist Convention has never taken an official position for or against the ordination of women. One might debate whether resolutions, often voted under time pressures to adjourn, really reflect the mind of the registered messengers, much less the millions of Southern Baptist church members back home. Nevertheless, after years of debate the SBC has refused to take any official position on this issue, or to direct its agencies for or against recognition or endorsement of ordained women. The Convention has left ordination with the local churches, where historically it has always been.

Neither has the SBC taken any official notice or disciplinary action against any affiliated church that has ordained women as ministers or deacons. Some local associations, however, have disciplined and even excluded churches for ordaining women.

Summary

Baptist women began the twentieth century unable to serve as messengers to the Southern Baptist Convention; now they serve as Convention officers, chair its committees, speak to its reports. Women may feel, understandably, that they have yet a long way to go. They have, however, already come a long, long way.

One rapidly emerging role for Southern Baptist women is that of ordained deacon. The next chapter will explore that development, looking at both historical and biblical arguments about women deacons.

Notes

[1] *SBC Annual,* 1929, 102.

[2] *Religious Herald,* May 16, 1929, 3.

[3] *SBC Annual,* 1919, 125-31.

[4] Norman Herbert Letsinger, *The Women's Liberation Movement: Implications for Southern Baptists* (Unpublished Ph.D. dissertation, Louisville, Southern Baptist Theological Seminary, 1973), 108.

[5] Ibid., 154, 320.

[6] *Maryland Baptist,* May 25, 1978, 3.

[7] Letsinger, 157.   [8] *SBC Annual,* 1923, 18.

[9] *SBC Annual,* 1963, 79.

[10] Louisville; Baptist Book Concern, 1923.

[11] J. W. Porter, *Feminism: Woman and Her Work* (Louisville: Baptist Book Concern, 1923), 7.

[12] Ibid., 41.   [13] Ibid., 25.   [14] Letsinger, 113.

[15] Juliette Mather, "Margaret Fund," *Encyclopedia of Southern Baptists,* ed. Norman W. Cox (Nashville: Broadman Press, 1958), II, 820.

[16] William Wright Barnes, *The Southern Baptist Convention 1845-1953* (Nashville: Broadman Press, 1954), 162.

[17] William Wright Barnes, "Southwestern Baptist Theological Seminary," *Encyclopedia of Southern Baptists* (Nashville: Broadman Press, 1958), II, 1282.

[18] *SBC Annual,* 1973, 87.

[19] *Western Recorder,* June 23, 1973, 8.

[20] *SBC Annual,* 1974, 208.

[21] Ibid., 210.   [22] Ibid., 62.

[23] *SBC Annual,* 1975, 56.

[24] *Western Recorder,* June 21, 1975, 11.

[25] *Rocky Mountain Baptist,* June 27, 1975, 1.

[26] *Baptist Message,* June 23, 1977, 1.

SEVEN

Women Deacons

The Deacons and Their Husbands

At first glance Jean Wright is not that unusual. She is an attractive, energetic wife and mother in Durham, North Carolina, whose husband is a city engineer. A former school teacher, Mrs. Wright is now active in the real estate business. Like all working wives, she has to juggle time for business and family, but she seems to have the inner strength and outward organization to make it work. Jean and her family are devout Southern Baptists, active in the Watts Street Baptist Church of Durham. At some time Jean has taught Sunday School, worked in WMU, and in every way taken as active a church role as job and family permit.

So far, not too unusual. With minor changes this could be the description of any one of thousands of Southern Baptist women. However, there is something more about Jean. She is an active deacon in her church, having been ordained in 1974. In 1976 she served a term as chairman of the deacon board. She describes it as a routine year, in which her leadership was accepted without incident. In 1978 she served as the stated moderator of her church business sessions. Of 24 active deacons at the Watts Street church in 1978, nine were women, some ordained back in the 1960's.

Jean Wright is an example of a mushrooming new role for Baptist women, that of church deacon. While exact numbers are not to be had, apparently some hundreds of Southern Baptist churches now ordain women deacons, and the number is growing rapidly. Perhaps the total number of Southern Baptist women deacons now runs into the thousands. This chapter will trace historically the origin and growth of this significant new role for Southern Baptist women.

No New Question

For Baptist women to serve as deacons is no new thing. We have seen that the earliest Baptist churches in England included "Deacons

Men, and Women," and early Baptist leaders acknowledged that "Deacons ar 1. men 2. weomen." [1] Nor was this merely theoretical, for local church records in England amply demonstrate that the woman deacon, or deaconess, was a fixture, especially in churches of the General Baptist persuasion. The more Calvinistic group, called Particular Baptists, allowed less active roles for women, in both England and America.

In colonial America some Baptist churches had deaconesses, and some even had a separate order of eldresses. Baptist churches in Europe have long acknowledged deaconesses, though this is less common among Baptist churches in Latin America.

Many who know of deaconesses among Baptists in England, Europe, and Colonial America may not be aware of the extent to which this has been an accepted office among Southern Baptists both in older and more contemporary times. In 1846, one year after the Southern Baptist Convention was formed, R. B. C. Howell published an important book on *The Deaconship, Its Nature, Qualifications, Relations, and Duties.* [2] Howell was a leading Southern Baptist, an architect of the Convention, and a writer of note whose influence among Southern Baptists was vast. His was one of the earliest books on the diaconate by a Southern Baptist, and it held sway until supplanted by the more restricted views of J. M. Pendleton a generation later. [3]

Howell shows from the New Testament that early churches had deaconesses, citing Scripture from Romans 16:1, 1 Timothy 5:9-10, 1 Timothy 3:11, and others. Howell concludes: "Take all these passages together, and I think it will be difficult for us to resist the conclusion that the word of God authorizes, and in some sense, certainly by implication, enjoins the appointment of deaconesses in the churches of Christ. . . . Deaconesses, therefore, are everywhere, as necessary as they were in the days of the apostles." [4]

As to the role of deaconesses, Howell argued that they were "female assistants to the deacons. . . . and their duty required them to minister to females, under circumstances in which it would have been manifestly improper that the other sex should have been employed." [5] While their moral qualifications were the same as for deacons, the deaconesses did have a different status in Howell's mind, for "deaconesses were not, as deacons are, formally ordained." [6]

Given Howell's status as a Southern Baptist leader and the wide-spread use of this book, one might have expected his views about deaconesses to prevail in the denomination. However, toward the end of his life Howell was involved in controversies which diminished his influence. Also Southern Baptist adverse reaction to the nine-teenth-century women's liberation movement tended to relegate women to more passive roles.

However, there are other indications of Southern Baptist sentiment in favor of deaconesses. In 1871 the influential *Religious Herald,* a Southern Baptist paper in Virginia, ran a guest editorial on "Minister-ing Women." In an introduction the editors commend the editorial, written by "L. M." of Kentucky, by saying: "We have long been convinced that our churches have failed to employ usefully their female members. They occupied a sphere of activity and usefulness in the apostolic churches, it seems to us, which has not been assigned to them in modern churches." [7]

The editorial itself reports on the successful work of women in other denominations. The writer suggests that each Baptist church should have deaconesses, and the larger ones should "set apart and sustain say two deaconesses" on the church payroll. They would visit the sick, minister to women and families, teach women the Bible and living skills, establish Sunday Schools for disadvantaged children, and enlist people to attend church. The fact that such an influential paper as the *Religious Herald* should endorse the idea of deaconesses as early as 1871 shows that the idea had wide accep-tance.

While not specifically advocating deaconesses, in 1865 Samuel Boy-kin, editor of the *Christian Index* of Georgia issued a strong article on "Female Influence in the Churches—Woman's Position." [8] He said that some have so emphasized the Pauline restrictions upon women that they have missed the positive side of the biblical message, and women have been in effect sidelined in the churches. "Thus," Boykin said, "has a mighty arm of strength been paralyzed, and a talent hidden so long that the churches are incredulous as to its real existence." [9]

Boykin cited the Pauline exhortation that women keep silent in the church, and showed how this passage was influenced by first-century culture. He also implied that this restriction cannot be ironclad, for he asked, What if a woman has no husband to ask at home? What if he is ungodly? or What if he did not attend church? Citing Bible passages portraying women as "servants of the church," "helpers in Christ Jesus," and "Laborers in the Lord," Boykin asked why modern women should not also serve these roles. He admitted that "the opinions of this age are against it. Teachers do not encourage it, pious husbands withhold their sanction, and the churches together with public sentiment do not approve."

Boykin insisted these reasons are not good enough, and concluded with a ringing appeal for more active roles for Baptist women. He said: "The eyes of the pious are now turning, more than on any former occasion, to godly women. The pastors need and greatly desire their cooperation; . . . the Sabbath Schools need them." [10]

Another indication of Southern Baptist interest in deaconesses came from J. R. Graves, sometimes called "the most influential Southern Baptist who ever lived." He was the primary founder of the Landmark movement, an ultraconservative movement among Southern Baptists in the nineteenth century. A onetime associate and later opponent of R. B. C. Howell, Graves exerted wide influence as editor of the *Tennessee Baptist,* a paper founded by Howell.

In an article on "Woman's Work in the Church," Graves said: "There is no doubt in the minds of Biblical and ecclesiastical scholars, that in the apostolic churches women occupied the office of the deaconship. . . . Phoebe was a deaconess of the church in Cenchrea." [11]

Graves concluded that "There is no good reason why saintly women should not fill the office of deaconess to-day in most churches. In fact, they often perform the duties of the office without the name." [12] Graves seemed genuinely sympathetic to Baptist women who wanted to serve their Lord, suggesting also that they could be active in missions, Sunday School work, and private charity. He did, however, specifically rule the pulpit off-limits to women.

With books and Baptist papers advocating deaconesses, it is not surprising that the question was widely discussed and debated. For example, at the Baptist State Convention in Waxahachie, Texas, in 1884, one of the first agenda items for debate was, "Do the Scriptures Authorize the Appointment of Women as Deaconesses?" [13] Unfortunately, we do not know what was said about the issue, and the convention records no action taken. The fact that it came up at all shows that the question was current at that time, but perhaps the form of the question shows that Baptist understanding was divided.

However, this was not merely a theory to be discussed. Evidence suggests that numerous Southern Baptist churches did indeed have deaconesses in the nineteenth and into the twentieth centuries. For example, in 1877 the First Baptist Church of Waco, Texas, set aside six deaconesses and specified their duties. Dr. B. H. Carroll was pastor of this church from 1871 to 1899, and afterward was founder of the Southwestern Baptist Theological Seminary in Fort Worth, Texas. Though he acknowledged deaconesses as a biblical office, Carroll was unwilling for them to exercise any real leadership. Throughout his pastorate, the church manual "Rules of Decorum" specified that "It shall be the duty of every free male member to attend each and every conference" of the church. [14]

The Third Baptist Church of St. Louis is another church that has long had deaconesses. Affiliated with both Southern and Northern Baptist conventions, the Third Church from early times had a Board of Deaconesses to match the Board of Deacons. By 1950 this church had 60 deaconesses, described as "a tremendous asset to the church." [15]

The evidence suggests that in the nineteenth century many Southern Baptists approved deaconesses and regarded the offices as biblical. Moreover, at least some churches acted upon these views and regularly set aside deaconesses as well as deacons. Probably Southern Baptist churches have never been without deaconesses. Though somewhat in decline, the acceptance of deaconesses persisted into the present century. One finds numbers of Southern Baptist churches with deaconesses in the 1920's and 1930's, and of course recently the practice is being revived.

If Southern Baptists regarded deaconesses as biblical, why did the office decline? Charles DeWeese, a Baptist historian who has made a study of this question, suggests changes in the nature of the diaconate is responsible. He points out that in the early years the deacon and deaconess ministered directly to people's needs, but gradually the work of the Baptist deacon shifted from ministry to management. He says "the diaconal function began to be viewed more and more in administrative, business, and management categories to the neglect of the more caring and supporting ministries." [16]

Since women in America were not generally involved in management, the churches were unwilling to put them into this role. The office of deaconess declined therefore because the office of deacon changed from ministry to management. Part of the recent revival of deaconesses and women deacons may be a result of a shift back toward the ministering concept of deacons.

A Practice Revived

In May, 1972, deacons from Baptist churches throughout Virginia gathered for a conference about the work of the deaconship. Noticing a number of women in the group, the conference leader welcomed them as "wives of deacons." Gently but firmly the women pointed out that they were at the conference as full-fledged deacons from their churches.

This experience is just a sample of what is happening to the diaconate in Baptist churches. No longer is the board of deacons an all-male preserve. Scores of Southern Baptist churches now have women deacons, and not a few have elected women to chair the deacon group. A number of churches have adopted bylaws to require that 50 percent of the active deacons be women. While such churches are relatively few among the 34,000 Southern Baptist churches, the trend is unmistakable.

While this practice seemed to mushroom in the early 1970's, Southern Baptist churches have had women deacons for a long time. In a 1973 survey of churches with women deacons, *The Deacon,* a publication of the Sunday School Board of the SBC, reported that some churches had women deacons at least by the 1920's. For example, the Wake Forest Church in North Carolina reportedly has had women deacons since 1924. The Danville Church in Georgia reportedly ordained a woman deacon in 1931. The chairman of deacons at the First Baptist Church in Decatur, Georgia, in 1978 was a woman who was first ordained in 1952. Several North Carolina churches in 1978 still had living women deacons who had been chosen before World War I.

Most women deacons, however, have been ordained since 1965. Sometimes church leaders have suggested this step; at other churches women have been nominated from the floor. Since many churches list only "males over twenty-one" as eligible for election as deacons, some problems were created when women's names showed up among nominees. While some churches simply discarded the ineligible names, others were provoked to study the issue. The result has been that a number of churches voted to remove the "men only" requirements.

While exact numbers are not to be had, it was estimated in 1973 that two to three hundred Southern Baptist churches had women deacons or deaconesses.[17] No doubt the number has grown since then. By 1976 Virginia Baptists alone reported 520 women deacons and deaconesses in 57 churches.[18] Other states with a large number of women deacons include North Carolina, South Carolina, Georgia, Tennessee, and Texas. While the largest number of women deacons are in churches in the Southeast, they are not unknown in churches throughout Convention territory.

Deacon and Deaconess

Is there a difference between women deacons and deaconesses? Confusion arises because some churches use the same terms but with different meanings.

Some use "deacon" and "deaconess" to designate men and women who have the same status, serve on the same board, and perform the same duties in the church. For them the terms designate the same function, like "waiter" and "waitress," with the only difference being sex. In this usage, deacons and deaconesses are elected and ordained in the same way.

Others use the terms quite differently. By "deacon" they designate the men who are elected and ordained by the church, who deal with administrative and policy recommendations to the church, and who help administer the Lord's Supper. By "deaconess" they designate a separate and subordinate group of women who are appointed, not ordained, and who minister mostly to women and children in the church. For those who use the term in this way, a deaconess would have nothing to do with administration or church policy, and certainly would not help serve the Lord's Supper.

Churches today which report having women as deacons or deaconesses do not usually clarify how they use the term. Some churches that report having "women deacons" fifty or more years ago, upon closer examination, apparently had deaconesses in the subordinate sense.

Whether deaconess in the New Testament designates an order of women separate from the deacons, or whether deacon and deaconess were merely masculine and feminine forms to designate the same office, scholars still debate. At any rate, it is clear that in early Baptist history in England the women were deacons in the full sense of that word. Only later did the deaconess concept develop among English Baptists. The deaconess, for most of Baptist history, has had different duties and a status distinctly inferior to men deacons.

The same is true of Baptists in America. Even among the Separate Baptists of the South, where deaconesses were quite customary, they occupied a distinctly different status than men deacons. The Southern Baptist leaders quoted earlier in this chapter as approving of deaconesses did just that—approve of *deaconesses* in the subordinate sense of that word. This is amply illustrated in the influential book on *The Deaconship* by R. B. C. Howell, who says that the office of deaconess is biblical, but they are optional and are merely appointed rather than ordained.[19] In many churches today women on benevolence and baptism committees often serve much the same function as Baptist deaconesses once served.

Recent developments, however, mark a significant shift in the status of women set apart for the diaconate. For the most part, Baptist churches today are not appointing deaconesses in the subordinate sense of that word, but women deacons who are elected, ordained, and assigned the same duties as men. Women deacons today do whatever deacons do, whether administration, policy recommendations, or serving the Lord's Supper. They meet with the deacons, rather than in separate groups as deaconesses usually do. In short, today's Southern Baptist woman deacon is a *deacon* in the fullest sense.

Why Women Deacons?

At times Southern Baptist churches would not even allow women to vote in church; now they are ordaining women as deacons. What are the reasons for this change in the role of women? What factors explain the spectacular upsurge in the number of women deacons among Southern Baptists?

One can rarely say for sure why anything happens. The historian can at most suggest some contributing factors. That is certainly the case in seeking to explain the new openness to women deacons. However, one may cite such contributing factors as changes in society, the example of other denominations, new dimensions of Bible study, new thoroughness of historical research, and certain practical considerations.

Women, as well as men, have been affected by sweeping changes in American society in the past century. Better education means our daughters are as well-informed and prepared as our sons. Family planning and fewer children mean that women have more freedom to look beyond home and hearth for challenge and fulfillment. The industrial revolution thrust women into jobs outside the home, and modern economy almost mandates their continued employment. Technology has cut down the time and physical effort of housework.

The secular women's liberation movement certainly affected church women, both in the nineteenth century and the twentieth. One should not be surprised that what happens in society affects the church, for church people live, hold jobs, rear children, and balance budgets in the same world. Nor is this a new thing. In every age, major events in the secular world have had their influence in the church.

Another factor in the acceptance of women deacons is a new understanding of the Bible. Southern Baptists accept the authority of the Bible, and they always have. Nothing is more characteristic of them than their fierce allegiance to the Word of God, as they understand it. However, their understanding of some passages may change from one generation to the next. In the nineteenth century many Southern Baptists understood the Bible in such a way as to keep women in silence and subjection, a distinctly inferior role in the church.

Recently, however, a growing number of Southern Baptists are reading the same passages in a different light. They discover in both testaments an emphasis upon human dignity and equality. Even the most restrictive biblical statements about women take on new dimensions when interpreted in context, and in light of the teachings and practices of Jesus. It is a fact of far-reaching significance that a growing number of Southern Baptist pastors, scholars, and laypeople no longer interpret the Bible as excluding modern women from an active role in religion.

Obviously one's cultural inheritance will influence his interpretation of the Bible. One might argue that the nineteenth-century Southern Baptist was culturally conditioned to find in the Bible authority to subordinate women, and that today's reader is conditioned by a changing society to find biblical authority to liberate women. Southern Baptist allegiance to the Bible is unchanging. Their interpretation, however, seems to be changing, at least on the role of women in religion.

A new intensity of historical research is another factor in the increased role of church women, including Southern Baptists. For generations some histories of Christianity have almost ignored women as if they did not exist. Modern studies, however, are rediscovering the other half of the human race. We now know that churchwomen were not silent and sidelined for twenty centuries. Modern women insist they are but reasserting some of their historic precedents and prerogatives.

The example of other denominations has not escaped the attention of Southern Baptist women. Just as their formation of Woman's Missionary Union in the past century was influenced to some extent by similar groups among women of other denominations, Southern Baptist women have been acutely aware of the role of women among other Baptist groups and in American churches generally. Many other Baptist groups ordained women as deacons and ministers long before Southern Baptists did.

However valid these may be as contributing factors, perhaps more immediate practical matters have shaped Baptist developments in the role of women. More than half of the church membership and attendance at the typical Southern Baptist church is female. Women have long been in the forefront of the church's teaching, enlistment, and giving programs. It is a common saying among Baptists that without the women the churches would fall dead. Today's Baptist woman may be better educated, better informed about the church and its needs, better equipped to work with people, and more deeply committed to Christ than most men. In that case, some are asking, is it fair for half the people to be unrepresented on the deacon board? Some even suggest it may be necessary to admit women to leadership roles in order to retain the allegiance and participation of women newly aware of their own potential.

Reactions to Women Deacons

Almost without exception, Southern Baptist churches that have ordained women as deacons report that the experience has been beneficial beyond all expectations. One church in North Carolina was reported to have rescinded an earlier vote to ordain women: most churches that ordain women regard the change as an unqualified success. Reports that women make effective deacons and that churches that have them are benefited, not destroyed, may have more to do with growth of the practice than theology.

However, beyond such surface problems as how to address a woman who chairs the deacon group ("chairman," "chairwoman," "chairperson"), and whether women deacons and deaconesses have the same office, other problems remain. As on most issues, Southern Baptists are sharply divided on the validity of the deacon role for women.

Many Southern Baptists oppose the idea of women deacons on the basis of the Bible and theology. Those who hold this view often point out that Acts 6:3 says "look ye out among you seven men," not seven women. Another favorite verse for opponents is 1 Timothy 3:12, which says, "Let the deacons be the husband of one wife." One opponent said: "Women as deacons in the church is contrary [sic] to Bible teaching, as found in 1 Timothy 3:11. The qualifications for deacons are outlined in 1 Timothy 3:8-12. One qualification is that a deacon should be the husband of one wife. This excludes women." [20]

Generally, those who oppose women deacons regard the "wives" of 1 Timothy 3:11 as the wives of the deacons. Those who hold this view also point to such passages as 1 Corinthians 14:34-35 and 1 Timothy 2:11-15. The first passage admonishes women to keep silent in the church at Corinth, and if they want more information to ask their own husbands at home. The latter passage is similar but adds that women may not teach or exercise authority over men, but must remain in silence. Opponents also point to the practice of Jesus who chose twelve apostles, all men. Not many, even among those who oppose leadership roles for women, would go so far as one man who settled the entire question by pointing out, "God sent His son to save the world. He did not send His daughter."

Those who accept the role of women as deacons also use Scripture and theology, often the very same passages, differently interpreted. Some biblical scholars regard the "seven men" of Acts 6:3 as a benevolence committee, rather than the origin of deacons. As to 1 Timothy 3:12, "let the deacons be the husbands of one wife," some interpret this to mean a prohibition of polygamy. Church officers, including deacons, might be married but to only one spouse. According to this view, Paul used the masculine to illustrate the principle, but it would be equally valid to say, "Let the deacons be the wives of one husband." Moreover, a literal interpretation of this text would disqualify a single man or widower from the deaconship, which few churches do.

Some who favor women deacons interpret 1 Corinthians 14:34-35 and 1 Timothy 2:11-15 as timely instructions for those local churches, given to deal with specific problems which had arisen at that time and place. According to this view, these statements are not necessarily intended to be binding upon all women of all times. One pastor who had just ordained women deacons said, "While there are biblical statements indicating inferiority of women to men, I could understand these passages as vestiges of first century culture." [21]

Proponents also point to such passages as Romans 16:1, which refers to Phoebe as a deaconess. Some English versions, including the familiar King James Version, translate this as "servant," but other translations follow the Greek which has the word for deaconess. Many also point out that in 1 Timothy 3:11 the word used is not "wives," but "women," and thus may refer to a separate group of women deacons. The "elder women" of 1 Timothy 5:2 and the "widow" of 1 Timothy 5:9 suggest to some interpreters that the New Testament churches may have had specific orders for women much like deacons or deaconesses of today.

Neither those who oppose women deacons nor those who favor will be satisfied with these summaries. This book is primarily historical, to set out what has happened and what is happening. To advocate or defend this or that position, and to seek to justify it by Scripture, is no part of the intent here. However, this brief summary of at least some arguments on both sides seems necessary to complete the picture.

It appears that Southern Baptist women deacons are here to stay. All evidence suggests the practice is growing rapidly. While opposition is still prevalent, voices of acceptance and defense are increasing in number and volume.

This probably means some changes in the historic role of Baptist deacons. For most of the twentieth century the deacons have been regarded, and regarded themselves, more or less as the board of managers of a Baptist church. Visitation, enlistment, and ministry to those in need has at times almost been lost from sight. However, there seems to be a move today to recover the ministry of the diaconate. Perhaps the ordination of women as deacons will help recover the caring aspect of their work.

There may also be other changes. For decades the annual deacons' party, usually around Christmas time, has seen invitations worded, "to the deacons and their wives." Might not the future see invitations saying also, "to the deacons and their husbands?"

Notes

[1] William L. Lumpkin, *Baptist Confessions of Faith* (Valley Forge: Judson Press, 1959), 121; William T. Whitely, ed. *The Works of John Smyth* (Cambridge: University Press, 1915), I, 259.

[2] Philadelphia: American Baptist Publication Society, 1846.

[3] J. M. Pendleton, *Church Manual Designed for the Use of Baptist Churches* (Nashville: Sunday School Board of the Southern Baptist Convention, n.d.).

[4] R. B. C. Howell, *The Deaconship,* 104-105.

[5] Ibid., 98.   [6] Ibid., 107-108.

[7] *Religious Herald,* April 13, 1871, 1.

[8] *Christian Index,* April 13, 1865, 2.

[9] Ibid.   [10] Ibid.

[11] *The Baptist,* February 22, 1879.

[12] Ibid.

[13] Minutes of the Thirty-Seventh Annual Session of the Baptist State Convention of Texas, October 4-6, 1884, 53.

[14] Frank Burkhalter, *A World-Visioned Church* (Nashville: Broadman Press, 1946), 100, 300.

[15] Norman E. Nygaard, *Where Cross the Crowded Ways* (New York: Greenberg, 1950), 185.

16 Charles W. Deweese, "Deaconesses in Baptist History: A Preliminary Study," *Baptist History and Heritage* (January, 1977), 54-55.

17 *The Deacon* (April–June, 1973), 14.

18 Report of the Christian Life Committee to the Baptist General Association of Virginia, 1976, 22b.

19 Howell, 107-108.

20 *The Deacon* (April–June, 1973), 9.

21 *Baptist Courier,* February 28, 1974.

EIGHT

Women as Ministers

Your Daughters Shall Prophesy

On August 9, 1964, Addie Davis was ordained as a gospel minister at the Watts Street Baptist Church in Durham, North Carolina. So far as the record indicates, she was the first woman formally ordained by a Southern Baptist church. This set in motion new trends which have far-reaching significance for Baptists and their concepts of ministry.

A native of Covington, Virginia, Miss Davis graduated from two Southern Baptist schools, Meredith College and Southeastern Baptist Theological Seminary. From the seminary she received her Bachelor of Divinity in 1963, the standard theological degree for ministry. At the time of her ordination, Davis was no stranger to church work. She had previously served as assistant pastor of First Baptist Church of Elkins, North Carolina, and as Dean of Women at Alderson-Broaddus College in West Virginia. She had also served as supply pastor at the Lone Star Baptist Church in her hometown of Covington, Virginia. After her ordination, she became pastor of the First Baptist Church of Readsboro, Vermont.[1]

Warren Carr, pastor of the Watts Street Church in 1964, said the ordination of Davis "was almost solely due to her personal testimony. We took her seriously when she said that God had called her to the ordained ministry and that she could not rest until she answered that call."[2]

This ordination raised a storm of protest from Southern Baptists who regarded it as contrary to Scripture. However, the furor soon quieted because no other ordinations followed in the immediate future. Also criticism was blunted somewhat by the fact that Davis accepted a pastorate outside of Southern Baptist life. Most Baptists respected the autonomy of the Watts Street Church whether or not agreeing with its actions.

In this chapter we will look at the issue of ministerial ordination for women and sketch briefly the stories of some of those ordained. We will also seek to assess their opportunities and problems in ministry, explore the meaning of this new trend, and cite some reactions from Southern Baptists.

Daughters Who Prophesy

An Old Testament prophet looked toward a time when "your sons and your daughters shall prophesy" (Joel 2:28). Southern Baptists have long been accustomed for their sons to prophesy (preach), but it is still unusual for their daughters to do so. However, a number of Baptist daughters as well as sons have professed a call to ministry and have sought ordination. Between 1964 and 1978 perhaps fifty or more women have been ordained in Southern Baptist churches. While many of these serve in chaplaincy, counseling, and teaching positions, a number are in pastoral and preaching roles. In addition to those known to be ordained already, there were in 1977 more than 1,600 women enrolled in SBC theological seminaries.[3] Many of them say they intend to seek ordination upon graduation. Therefore, what began in 1964, and was not repeated until 1971, may become in the future a major trend in Southern Baptist ministry.

The following list of ordained women was compiled by Helen Lee Turner, who was ordained in 1975 in South Carolina. Since no SBC agency collects this information, Turner sifted it primarily from Baptist press releases and personal correspondence.

Adams, Camile	Crawford, Julienne
Applewhite, Octavia	Davis, Addie
Bailey, Marjorie Lee	Davis, Betty
Bishop, Susan	Davis, Suzanne Martin
Blackwell, D. Claire	Denham, Susan Sprague
Boyle, Elizabeth Hutchens	Denham, Priscilla Lane
Brannon, Victoria Jean	Dotson, LaNell
Buckner, Brenda	Dowd, Sharyn E.
Carter, Sallie Amanda	Duvall, Pearl Holmes
Carter, Shirley	Fitzgerald, Sue
Cowell, Vicki	Fordham, Druecillar
Coyle, Suzanne	Forehand, Mary Ann

Forrester, Donna
Fusilier, Aliene
Galphin, Lillian Wells
Gilmore, Martha Niendorff
Grady, Hazel
Hargis, Esther
Hickman, Elaine
Hill, Diane E.
Johnson, Brenda Carol
   Jowers
Johnson, N. Joy
Johnson, Pamela Jean
Kneece, Brenda Lynn
Laidlaw, Marysusan Nance
Lawrence, Lana
Macon, Arlene Westbrook
Metzger, Geneva Nell
Neill, Meredith Whitefield

Phillips, Jeanette Zachry
Pruett, Jean S.
Pruett, Linda Jean
Rhymer, Susan
Rosser, Anne Plunkett
Schlegel, Elizabeth Anne
   Haskins
Scott, Sharon S.
Smith, Kay
Smith, Libby Bellinger
Smith, Nancy Lyons
Stafford, Margaret Ann
Stanton, Nancy Layne
Thom, Kathline
Tiller, Nell Alrede
Turner, Helen Lee
Watson, Susan
Wisemiller, Dianne

Doubtless there are others not included in this list, including some previously ordained and some ordained while this book was being printed. This does not take account, either, of that vast number of Southern Baptist women who are doing the work of ministry without formal ordination. While space does not allow a full biographical sketch of each of these, perhaps a bit more information about some of them would be appropriate.

After the ordination of Addie Davis in 1964 there was not another ordination of a woman until 1971, when the Kathwood Baptist Church in Columbia, South Carolina, ordained Shirley Carter. However, in 1972 the Kathwood church voted to rescind this ordination, making Miss Carter the only Southern Baptist woman known to have relinquished her ordination.

Marjorie Lee Bailey, the third woman ordained by Southern Baptists, had been for six years a chaplain at the Virginia State Industrial Farm. A mature woman with years of experience, she was ordained in February, 1972, at the Bainbridge Street church in Richmond. During the ordination, George Ricketts, director of the Chaplain Service of the Churches of Virginia, said, "Forgive us for so long delaying this act which recognizes you in the fullest sense as a minister of the gospel." [4]

Before becoming a chaplain, Bailey was for 15 years director of the South Richmond Baptist Center. She has also worked in riverfront missions in New Orleans. She graduated from Blue Mountain College in Mississippi, and attended Southwestern Baptist Theological Seminary in Fort Worth. Of her ordination she says, "it was just something I felt the Lord had called me to do." [5] Her experiences in prison chaplaincy and a year of Clinical Pastoral Education in Virginia convinced her that ordination would add a dimension to her ministry. However, she disclaimed any notion of starting a trend among Southern Baptists. Scattered opposition to her ordination was expressed in the Richmond Baptist Association, but most supported her decision.

Marjorie Bailey's ministerial career has been distinguished. The first Southern Baptist woman ordained in Virginia, she was in 1977 promoted to senior chaplain for the Virginia State Penitentiary. She was the first female chaplain of any denomination in America to hold such an appointment. [6]

Perhaps the senior minister among Southern Baptist women is Druecillar Fordham of New York City. She was ordained in 1942 among National Baptists, and has been pastor of the Christ Temple Baptist Church in Harlem since 1963. In 1972 this church was received into fellowship with the Metropolitan Baptist Association, the Southern Baptist association of New York City. Though not ordained among Southern Baptists, this makes Fordham, a widow, the first woman pastor of a Southern Baptist church.

Admitting that some have opposed her ministry, Fordham loves to quote Galatians 3:28 that all are one in Christ. Regarding opposition to women clergy, she says she does not defend her role. "I haven't got time for a lot of that kind of foolishness any more," she says. "I never fear anything. I just go ahead and do it. People will say what they want to say; they have a right to—but it doesn't matter. We're living in the *now* age." [7] She says she has been warmly received by the pastors in the Metropolitan Association.

The first woman employee of a Southern Baptist Convention agency to be ordained was Elizabeth G. Hutchens, a member of the faculty at Southern Baptist Theological Seminary in Louisville.

While on a sabbatical leave in Virginia, Hutchens served as a chaplain intern at Saint Elizabeth's Hospital. Federal regulations require ordination for those who hold this position, so her home church, Crescent Hill in Louisville, requested her ordination. She was ordained by Baptist Temple in Alexandria, Virginia. Later she returned to her post as associate professor of religious education at Southern Seminary.[8]

The first woman ordained in Texas, and perhaps the ninth in Southern Baptist Convention, was Jeanette Zachry. She was ordained in 1974 by the Broadway Baptist Church of Fort Worth upon her graduation from Southwestern Seminary. Her intention was to seek appointment as a military chaplain, a position which requires ordination.

The ordination of Hazel Grady of Decatur, Georgia, is unusual in that she did not at first request it. A church committee, which made a sweeping study of the total ministry of the church, recommended ordination for several staff positions in order to spotlight that these were "ministry" too. A longtime staff member at the Oakhurst church in Decatur, Grady accepted ordination in 1974.

Susan Sprague was ordained by the Willow Meadows Baptist Church in Houston in late December, 1975. A graduate of Vanderbilt University and a 1976 graduate of Southern Baptist Theological Seminary, Sprague sought ordination to work as a campus minister. She had previously worked under the US-2 program of the Home Mission Board, had been a youth director, and had served an internship in campus ministry at Yale University, a work sponsored jointly by the Maryland Baptist Convention and Southern Seminary. Pastor Ralph Langley of the Willow Meadows church said the church voted 84 percent in favor of the ordination, and the ordaining council voted 14-1 in favor.[9]

Perhaps Darryl and Aldrede Tiller of Georgia were the first ordained married couple in Southern Baptist life. Darryl, an alumnus of Southern Seminary, was ordained first. His plan was to enter the pastorate. Aldrede was ordained in 1977 by the First Baptist Church of Rockmart, Georgia. She served later as principal chaplain at Hazelwood Hospital in Louisville. Two other ordained women shared in her ordination service, Hazel Grady and Pearl Duvall.[10]

Another ordained couple serve as copastors of the Twenty-Third and Broadway Baptist Church in Louisville. John Sylvester and his wife Joy Johnson are both Master of Divinity graduates of Southern Baptist Theological Seminary. She elected to retain her maiden name to preserve her own individuality and identity as copastor of the church. She was ordained in 1977, and takes her regular turn preaching as well as performing all other duties associated with a Baptist pastorate. This church also has a number of women deacons, one of whom was chairman of the pulpit committee which recommended calling Sylvester and Johnson.

Considerable controversy was raised by the ordination of Martha Gilmore by the Cliff Temple Baptist Church of Dallas in 1977. The pastor of this second largest Baptist church in Dallas, A. Douglas Watterson, said the church "acted in the liberating spirit of the Gospel." [11] Mrs. Gilmore, a hospital chaplain in Dallas, had been a member of the Cliff Temple church since childhood. Considerable publicity was given to her ordination when W. A. Criswell, pastor of First Baptist Church in Dallas, spoke out in sharp opposition. A graduate of Baylor University, Martha and her husband Jerry, a Dallas attorney, have three children. She is currently working on a Master of Divinity degree at the Perkins School of Theology in Dallas, where she accepted a faculty position in 1978.

Kathline Thom was apparently the first Southern Baptist woman ordained to ministry in Missouri. She was ordained by the Wyatt Park Baptist Church in St. Joseph on August 28, 1977. Thom grew up in this church and later attended Southern Seminary in Louisville and Midwestern Seminary in Kansas City. Describing her ordination as a "natural step," she said, "God called me into the ministry, and ordination seemed like the natural response, just like baptism is the natural response for one who becomes a Christian."

The Wyatt Park pastor, Ernest White, pointed out that the church had encouraged Thom toward ministry since high school days. "We approved Kathy for Southern Seminary and for Midwestern Seminary. Ordaining her to the gospel ministry was a natural event. It was what she had prepared for, what the seminaries had prepared her for." [12]

Thom said she first felt a call to missions through the Girl's Auxiliary program in her church. She later served as a summer missionary in New Mexico and in several church staff positions, including associate Baptist Student Union campus minister for Missouri Western College. She hopes to become a full-time chaplain in a hospital. Her pastor said, "Ordination is necessary for Kathy to become a certified chaplain. But we did not ordain her so she could become a chaplain. We ordained her because we believe God has called her into the ministry." [13]

In the summer of 1978 Suzanne Martin Davis was elected associate director of student field ministries at the Southeastern Baptist Seminary in Wake Forest. She was previously ordained, and is thought to be the first woman already ordained to be employed by any SBC agency. A graduate of Meredith College, Davis also holds the Master of Divinity degree from Duke University. She will work with a team of professors and staff members to implement the newly developed Formation in Ministry program at Southeastern Seminary.

These are just a few of the women who have been ordained since 1964. The second ordination did not occur until 1971, with two in 1972, and three in 1973. Thereafter, the tempo increased, with eight women ordained in 1974. The numbers have increased rapidly since then.

Some mention should be made of the vast number of Southern Baptist women who routinely perform the work of ministry without ordination. It would be grossly misleading to convey the impression that Southern Baptist women have been active in ministry only since 1964, or that only fifty or so are engaged in ministry. For years Southern Baptist women have served as chaplains, counselors, ministers of education, ministers of music, and denominational workers without benefit of formal ordination. Perhaps a dozen or more unordained Southern Baptist women serve as Superintendents of Missions, a role usually held by men.

Perhaps many women would agree with Anna Marie Feltner, minister of education at First Baptist Church, Decatur, Georgia, who said, "When I entered the education ministry it was unheard of for women to be ordained. . . . I will not ask for ordination. My people know I am their minister." [14]

Suzanne M. Coyle, Minister

Any one of the women ordained to ministry by Southern Baptists might be singled out for more extensive treatment in this book. Suzanne Coyle has been chosen because more than some of the others, her ordination captured Baptist attention and triggered a definite Southern Baptist response.

Suzanne Coyle was reared as an only child in a devout Baptist family near Gravel Switch, Kentucky. Converted as a child, she was baptized into the Beech Fork Baptist Church of Gravel Switch. Her spiritual nurture was that of millions of Southern Baptist girls—revival meetings, Sunday School, Girl's Auxiliary mission groups, and of course regular preaching services.

As a high school student, Suzanne became interested in the ministry. Gradually the impression of God's call became more clear, and she switched her college major from music and psychology to religion. After graduation from Centre College in Danville, Kentucky, Miss Coyle entered Princeton Theological Seminary, where she earned a Master of Divinity degree in Pastoral Theology. She was in the honors program at Princeton. Her honors thesis, directed by Dr. Seward Hiltner, was entitled "Church Commitment Among Select Southern Baptist Women." Her record at Princeton was outstanding, as evidenced by the fact she was awarded a fellowship to return for advanced study.

Though no militant crusader in women's causes, Miss Coyle realized that ordination is the standard certification for ministers. If she expected to be accepted as a minister and function effectively in that role, ordination was essential. Therefore, she requested her home church of Beech Fork to ordain her.

The Beech Fork pastor and people realized, of course, that this was more than a routine ordination. They consulted with a number of people, including several professors at the Southern Baptist Theological Seminary in Louisville. In the end, however, they made their own decision based upon their knowledge of Suzanne and her commitment. They concluded that she had the necessary gifts and training for ministry and sensed in her life an authentic call from God. She was already active in ministry, serving as chaplain-pastor of the Center City Baptist Chapel in Philadelphia, a work sponsored jointly by the Paoli Baptist Church of Paoli, Pennsylvania, and the Home Mission Board of the Southern Baptist Convention. She also served as chaplain to the YMCA residence in which the chapel met.

Coyle was ordained in February, 1977, and reactions were not slow in developing. As early as February 14, 1977, the Executive Board of the South District Association of Baptists in Kentucky, with which the Beech Fork church was affiliated, took notice of the ordination and asked their Credentials Committee to investigate. In April the Executive Board "voted to recommend to the association in annual session that, unless Beech Fork Baptist Church rescended [sic] the ordination of Suzanne Coyle to the Gospel Ministry, that the association withdraw fellowship from that church." [15] The vote in the Executive Board was split 19 to 9. This gave the Beech Fork church scarcely six months until the annual session to rescind the ordination or face possible exclusion from an affiliation they had held for more than a century.

After consideration, the church decided to stand its ground. Members felt they were right in principle and also that this was an internal matter of that local congregation over which the association had no jurisdiction. Pastor Mike Jamison of the Beech Fork church said, "We don't plan to take any more action. We will not rescind Suzanne Coyle's ordination." [16]

In the months before the annual session each side lobbied for support. Beech Fork leaders pointed out that Miss Coyle was doing an outstanding job in her work and that ordination is a local church matter. Opponents, however, countered with arguments that ordination of women is unscriptural and that an association is within its rights to disfellowship churches for serious deviation.

At the annual session on October 17-18, 1977, several laymen of the Beech Fork church sought to explain their action and asked the group not to oust the 130-year-old church. A motion to refer the matter back to the Credentials Committee, which might have averted a final break, failed by the narrow margin of 92 to 80.[17] Upon the motion to exclude the Beech Fork church, the vote was 98 to 64, a clear majority. However, after the meeting, the moderator, Mike Moynahan, admitted that the group had agreed to conduct their official business in accord with *Roberts' Rules of Order.* This guide to parliamentary procedure requires a two-thirds majority to exclude, and the vote of the South District Association fell short of that. Therefore, there remains some doubt as to whether this was a binding vote to exclude, though all have so regarded it. The church may seek reinstatement to the association in the future.

After excluding the church that ordained her, the South District Association voted to send Miss Coyle a letter of encouragement. This letter, written by moderator Mike Moynahan, said in part:

"Although we disagree with what is surely one of the most significant choices of your life, we want you to know that we have not intended by this to convey any negative statement concerning your intended call to service or usefullness in the service of our Lord Jesus Christ. Our action was motivated by the majority's belief that both ordination and pastoral responsibility are Biblically inappropriate roles of service for any woman. We recognize you as our sister in Christ and wish through this letter to express our love and genuine concern for you. We recognize your wealth of talent and depth of commitment that may be used in a variety of appropriate roles. The discussion that resulted in this letter included the feeling that "the Lord might have something special" for you. I hope that the timing of our message does not do more harm than the good we intend. We do not want to wound you further. . . .

"Our sincere prayer for you is that our Lord might guide you, graceously [sic] care for your needs, and "let you do great things" which are in accord with His Devine [sic] Will for your ministry." [18]

The widespread publicity given to the Beech Fork exclusion elicited a number of letters pro and con. Many Baptist writers felt the association was well within its rights in excluding a church for what was regarded as violation of biblical teachings. Some wrote to the Home Mission Board, protesting any Convention agency sponsoring the work of an ordained woman. Officials of the Home Mission Board quickly pointed out that ordination was not a requirement for Coyle's work and that responsibility rested with the ordaining church, not the Home Mission Board. Other reactions to her ordination came from throughout the nation. Some of these will be cited later.

Meantime, Coyle continues her ministry, which involves counseling, pastoral visitation, and preaching. Those who know her are unanimous in their praise of her ability and commitment.

Why Here? Why Now?

The fact of women's ordination is clear, but the meaning of that fact requires more investigation. Why are Southern Baptists, who existed for generations with an all-male official ministry, now ordaining women?

One can rarely say for sure why anything happens. Often there are many causes for large trends and movements, and these causes may not be always easily identifiable. As for all such movements, simple explanations are suspect. However, perhaps some contributing factors can be pinpointed.

As in the case of women deacons, Southern Baptists have doubtlessly been influenced by changes in society which have given women more leadership roles. Women are more involved in American business, industry, education, and government. The world of religion, contrary to some opinion, is not insulated from the currents of life.

One should not think it strange that religion is affected by so-called "secular events," in this case the impact of the new roles of women in society. Throughout Christian history this interplay of church and culture has been evident. To some extent the shape of the early church, with its theology and ethics, was molded by the currents of the Graeco-Roman world. As Christianity, essentially a Jewish sect at first, moved into the larger Gentile world, its worship, structure, ministry, and theology were profoundly affected. The Protestant Reformation, though arising from deeper causes, was to some extent a response to economic, political, and social crises of the fifteenth and sixteenth centuries. Even a casual observer must be aware of the many ways Southern Baptists in this country have been shaped by frontier values and life-styles.

Therefore, one should be prepared for the fact that the newly emerging roles of Southern Baptist women are related to what is happening throughout American society. However, it is also true that the new roles of Baptist women go far beyond the influences of society.

One cannot account for the ordination of Baptist women, and indeed the entire new leadership of women in religion, apart from a revolution in biblical studies. In the past most Southern Baptists interpreted the Bible to keep women in silence and subjection. However, in recent years a growing number are reading these same biblical passages in a new light. They find in both testaments an emphasis upon human dignity and equality. Even the most restrictive biblical statements about women take on new dimensions when interpreted in context, and in light of the teaching and practice of Jesus. Right or wrong, many Southern Baptists today do not regard the Bible as preventing modern women from an active role in religion.

Aside from these arguments, other factors in women's ordination are more practical. Surrounded by the most pressing spiritual needs, such as crime, family disintegration, the undermining of moral standards, and spiritual decay on every hand, some ask why we should reject the help of half the human race.

Those who use this argument point out that women are often adept in counseling, teaching, caring ministries, and personal witnessing as well as the more formal ministerial roles of preaching and administering church programs. When the needs are here, and women have skills and dedication to help meet those needs, why should their help be refused?

Another factor encouraging the ordination of women is the success of women in ministry. Even those who oppose often admit the skills and effectiveness of women in ministry. There is a general feeling that women do make effective ministers, and may be superior to men in some kinds of ministry.

The recent proliferation of ordination for the nonpreaching ministry is another factor which has encouraged the ordination of women. A generation ago ordination was usually reserved for the preacher and deacon, and church staff workers in music and education were accounted as laymen. However, after World War II there was a widespread move to regard church music, church education, and other similar work as being part of the Christian "ministry" and as worthy of ordination as the preaching ministry. The result is that today one might be ordained to the ministry of music, education, childhood work, church business administration, youth work, or any number of other church vocations. Historically, women have performed a great deal of this kind of ministry. Now that these positions are eligible for ordination, more women are requesting ordination.

This change has both theological and practical overtones. A new and broader concept of "the ministry" has grown among Southern Baptists in recent years. However, the practical dimension is that the Internal Revenue Service allows substantial income tax advantages for ordained ministers. Baptists debate whether these advantages violate our concept of separation of church and state, but the fact remains that they are provided and most ministers legally take advantage of them. Before workers in church music, education, and youth were ordained, they could not qualify for these benefits. With ordination they can. While not a major factor, certainly, this cannot be overlooked in any assessment of the upsurge of ordination for women, and also for men.

In the final analysis, women want to be ordained because they want to be ministers. Many regard certification for ministers (that is, ordination) as necessary as proper certification for school teachers, doctors, or plumbers. This is especially so since many employment opportunities specify ordination as minimum qualification. Those ministers, men or women, who want to serve as chaplains in the military or in hospitals, or counselors in schools or other institutions, or campus ministers, or any number of other forms of employment, find that ordination is required. Without ordination they simply cannot be considered for these posts. This is certainly a powerful stimulus for ordination of women, since many women serve in these nonpastoral forms of employment.

After Ordination

The real struggle of Southern Baptist women who feel called to ministry is not in being ordained. The real struggle comes after ordination. With ordination papers in hand, women may ask themselves, what do I do now?

Unfortunately, some have been disappointed in ordination because it has not always opened the promised doors to fulfilling ministry. Some Southern Baptists women have found that ordination does not automatically abolish subordination. They still face the problems of being taken seriously as ministers, securing suitable employment, and receiving equitable salary benefits.

Without doubt, the major problem of ordained Southern Baptist women is securing suitable employment as ministers. Their problem is not unemployment, but underemployment. Many churches and denominational institutions would gladly employ capable women in subordinate helper roles. The trained woman can be a staff member in almost any church; in very few can she be pastor or even associate pastor. In Southern Baptist denominational agencies a majority of employees are women, but very few of them are at supervisory or managerial levels.

Most Southern Baptist women who have sought ordination are planning toward a ministry in chaplaincy, counseling, or teaching. Many say frankly that they do not aspire to the preaching or pastoral ministry. Perhaps some have accepted ordination not so much as fulfillment of a personal goal as to fulfill specific requirements for employment. Not only are Baptist women fulfilling some new roles, but some of the roles they have long filled now call for ordination. However, lest this be misunderstood, it should be clearly stated that other Baptist women do aspire to preaching and pastoral forms of ministry, and some are already in such positions.

After college, seminary, and ordination, some Baptist women show understandable flashes of bitterness at not finding suitable places of ministry. Usually they have been able to cope, however, and direct their energies to whatever task they find. Some have even found that second choice positions have turned into opportunities more exciting and challenging than first thought.

One young woman, ordained a few years ago, said: "When we started looking at places where the single woman can serve today; to be honest, it doesn't look very good." However, this young woman is now minister of education at a leading church in North Carolina. Traditionally, the single woman with a call to Christian service has gone to missions. However, in recent years opportunities for single women in missions, both home and foreign, have declined. Women at a Baptist conference asked, "If you're female, single, called to mission work, is there a place?" Some might answer in the negative. However, even they might be encouraged by a statement attributed to Cecil Etheredge of the Home Mission Board, who said:

"I think we must say to all our people that the young woman of today, single or married, must have the same freedom for Christian ministry as the man. I think it's a disservice to her if indeed we withold freedom to ministry from her, and offer it to a man just because history has so dictated." [19]

In addition to employment, women ministers face other problems. They want to be taken seriously as ministers. They weary of being regarded as freaks or fanatics, or "relative oddities," as one described them. Although comfortable with their own identity as women, they are tired of being endlessly described as "women ministers," and want to be just ministers.

Reactions to Women in Ministry

"What do you think about women as ministers?" That question will provoke a spirited discussion in almost any Southern Baptist group. Opinions may vary sharply from militant opponents to equally militant proponents. Perhaps a majority of Southern Baptists are somewhere in between, holding their own opinions but sometimes unsure whether they are valid. In this chapter we have set out some of the basic facts concerning women who have been ordained. We now look briefly at some reactions to those developments.

Some have found, not unexpectedly, that *women* have been among the primary opponents of newly emerging roles of Baptist women. Sue Fitzgerald encountered little opposition from men to her ordination in 1973, but says the women took longer to come around. She said, "Women had to change their views, but they came around after seeing me in action." Busy with preaching, marrying, burying, administering communion and teaching, Fitzgerald found people responded more positively to her *actions* as minister than to *arguments* about her ministry.[20]

However, some have not come around. Baptist associations and state conventions have passed resolutions expressing varying levels of disapproval of women's ordination. For example, the Executive Board of the Black River Association in Arkansas passed the following resolution March 15, 1976: "Bro. Marshal Link made motion to send letter to State Executive Secretary opposing the ordaining of Women. Motion seconed [sic] by Bro. John Eason. The Clerk of Black River Baptist Association to draw up the letter expressing the feelings of the Black River Baptist Association Executive Board against the ordination of women."[21]

The proposed letter was approved by the Executive Board and sent to Charles H. Ashcraft, executive secretary of the Arkansas Baptist Convention. Because this letter is of historical importance, and perhaps expresses the reactions of numerous Southern Baptists it seems good to quote it in some length. It was in response to the overall question of ordination of women, and specifically to some published statements of Dr. Ashcraft which some had interpreted as sympathetic to that practice. The letter said:

"Black River Baptist Associational Executive Board strongly oppose the articles printed in the Arkansas Baptist Newsmagazine concerning the ordination of women to the Gospel Ministry. The said articles was [sic] written by the Arkansas Baptist State Convention Executive Secretary. The said articles strongly emply [sic] and encourage the ordination of women. . . .

"The Arkansas Baptist State Convention Executive Secretary should not have such articles printed in our Baptist paper conveying the thought that most Southern Baptist Churches accept this view. *This* is not the case at all. This is and was only one man's opinion, the State Executive Secretary's.

"The Executive Board of Black River Baptist Association declare, and take an open stand in opposition to such an unbiblical doctrinal view. . . .

"We will encourage every church in our state to take a firm Biblical stand in the teaching of the Word of God, and shall encourage all churches to remain true to the guide lines laid down in the Word in Acts 6:1-7 and in I Tim. 3:1-13." [22]

Later the Arkansas state convention passed a similar resolution, adopted November 10, 1977. This resolution reads:

> WHEREAS, It has come to our attention that the Home Mission Board is giving financial support to an ordained woman; and
>
> Whereas, This is contradictory to the past practice of the Home Mission Board; and now be it
>
> THEREFORE RESOLVED, That the Arkansas Baptist State Convention meeting in Little Rock, Arkansas this November 10, 1977, go on record as looking with disfavor toward this practice; and be it
>
> FURTHER RESOLVED, That a copy of this resolution be sent to the Home Mission Board. [23]

At least one other association in Arkansas passed a similar resolution of opposition. The state convention resolution was probably aimed at Suzanne Coyle, who had recently been ordained in Kentucky but was ministering in Philadelphia in a mission sponsored in part by the Home Mission Board.

Earlier the Baptist General Convention of Oklahoma went on record as opposing the ordination of women as deacons or ministers. However, in Kentucky, where the Beech Fork church was ousted from its association for ordaining Coyle, the state convention refused to go along. In November, 1977, a messenger introduced a resolution of opposition, which emerged from the resolutions committee entitled "Resolution on Ordination of Women." However, the convention amended the wording to "Resolution on Ordination," without reference to sex or ministerial role, and voted the following resolution:

> Recognizing the historic position of Baptists (1) that Baptist ecclesiastical bodies do not exercise authority over the local church and (2) that individual churches exercise differing practices and beliefs about ordination for ministry;
> BE IT RESOLVED,
> 1. That the place of authority for ordination is centered in the authority of the local church under the authority of scripture. Churches ordain. Conventions do not.
> 2. That the recognition of the ordination and the utilization of those thus ordained is also the prerogative of the local church.[24]

This statement is important for its recognition of the autonomy of the local church and its disclaimer of any right or inclination for a convention to arbitrate internal church prerogatives.

An effort was made in Atlanta in 1978 to get the Southern Baptist Convention to vote on the question of ordination for women. However, such effort was ruled out of order and no vote was taken.

In addition to individuals and conventions, editors of some Baptist state papers have spoken out against ordination of women. Typical perhaps is an editorial appearing in *The Baptist Messenger* of Oklahoma, stating that:

"The Bible's teaching on the subject is so plain that it would seem unnecessary and a useless waste of time to discuss ordaining women as preachers or deacons in the churches. But evidently some individuals who call themselves Baptists and some churches affiliated with the Southern Baptist Convention are more interested in their own ideas on the subject than what the Scriptures have to say." [25]

Some well-known Southern Baptist pastors have spoken out

sharply against ordination of women. One Texas pastor said, "I am against it. Christ did not call one single woman to be one of his apostles." Another said, "I believe that women should hold all offices in the church wherein they can be in subjection to their own husbands." [26]

On the other side of the issue, some have spoken out in defense of ordination of qualified and called women. The Baptist Convention of Washington, D.C., voted to commend churches which had granted equality to qualified women in ministry. In an article "On Ordaining Women Bishops," Duke McCall concluded that while Baptists have no biblical precedents requiring us to ordain women, we have no specific biblical prohibition against it. This would apparently leave the issue at the initiative of each local church to assess the gifts and testimony of each person seeking ordination, whether men or women. McCall expressed what is perhaps a growing interpretation of Scripture passages, by saying: "Most Baptists have long since explained the admonitions to women to keep silent in the church as being rooted in an effort to calm a controversy in a local situation. It has not been understood by most Baptists as a universal injunction against female speech in church." [27]

One Baptist denominational leader who has spoken out on this issue in Charles H. Ashcraft, executive secretary of the Arkansas Baptist Convention. It would probably be inaccurate to say he has advocated the ordination of women, though his published articles have led some to that conclusion. Ashcraft has appealed for a spirit of openness and honesty in examining this new trend, and the biblical teachings that might apply. In a state where opposition to women's ordination has been strong, he has written articles, studied Scriptures, and perhaps most of all, asked questions which have forced Baptists to reexamine their stand.

In an article on "Women Preachers," Ashcraft points out biblical passages such as Joel 2:28-29 and Acts 21:19 which seem to imply that women preached in Bible times. He concluded that "At any point in history God can do what he predicted in Joel and confirmed by Peter. . . . and he will not ask for a convention resolution to do it." He also pointed out that most of our ordination practices grow out of tradition, not the Bible. Ashcraft concluded that: "Any lack of serious assessment of these delightful handmaidens of Al-

170

mighty God will not meet the smile of God." [28]

A similar theme was sounded by Jimmy Allen, president of the Southern Baptist Convention. In 1977 Allen said, when asked his view of women's ordination: "I am far more interested in expediting the contribution of women to sharing the Gospel than I am in the ceremonies of ordination. . . . God is obviously calling a great number of women into His service these days. Our seminaries are filled with them. The Bible is not a male-chauvinist document. I believe the burden of the message in the description of the role of the pastor in 1 Timothy was to set a standard of character and family stability rather than addressing the sex of the minister. I believe each local Baptist church, in keeping with our autonomy, will continue to search for the Holy Spirit's leadership and will do what is necessary to support these persons in their service to Christ." [29]

Southern Baptist opinion is sharply divided on the propriety of ordaining women as ministers. Perhaps many would agree with the man who wrote, "Women preachers would take some getting used to on my part—but why not?" [30]

Notes

[1] *Biblical Recorder,* August 15, 1964, 5.

[2] *Home Missions,* May, 1972, 26.

[3] Albert McClellan, *Meet Southern Baptists* (Nashville: Broadman Press, 1978), 64.

[4] *Home Missions,* May, 1972, 26.

[5] Ibid., 43.

[6] *Baptist Standard,* September 28, 1977, 12.

[7] *Home Missions,* May, 1972, 42.

[8] *Report from the Capitol,* May, 1973, 5.

[9] Baptist Press release, January 2, 1976.

[10] *Footprints,* Wayland Baptist College, October, 1977, 4.

[11] *Word and Way,* December 8, 1977, 5.

[12] Ibid., November 17, 1.

[13] Ibid.

[14] Baptist Press release, March 14, 1977.

[15] *Annual,* 1977, South District Association of Baptist in Kentucky, 15.

[16] Baptist Press release, May 4, 1977.

[17] *Annual,* 1977, South District Association of Baptist in Kentucky, 10.

[18] Personal letter from Mike Moynahan to Suzanne Coyle, February 9, 1977.

[19] *Home Missions,* July–August, 1976, 19.

[20] Baptist Press release, March 14, 1977.

[21] Minutes of Executive Board of Black River Baptist Association, March 15, 1976.

[22] Letter from Black River Baptist Association Executive Board to Charles H. Ashcraft, July 19, 1976.

[23] *Annual,* 1977, Arkansas Baptist State Convention, 44.

[24] *Western Recorder,* November 23, 1977, 6.

[25] *Baptist Messenger,* May 4, 1972, 2.

[26] *Baptist Program,* February, 1970, 25.

[27] *The Tie,* July–August, 1974, 3.

[28] *Arkansas Baptist,* December 4, 1975, 2.

[29] *Word and Way,* December 8, 1977, 5.

[30] *Baptist Program,* February, 1970, 25.

NINE

Whither Bound?

The Baptist Woman Tomorrow

Gladys S. Lewis gave the keynote address at the Consultation on Women in Church-Related Vocations at Nashville, September 22, 1978. Sponsored by various agencies of the Southern Baptist Convention, this was the first national meeting of Southern Baptist women to consider their opportunities and obstacles in ministry. Many observers would agree that Mrs. Lewis' address on "Awake, Deborah, Arise," helped set the tone not only for this meeting, but perhaps also for the future direction of Southern Baptist women.

A former missionary under the Foreign Mission Board, Lewis has held various denominational posts, including serving as a trustee for Southwestern Baptist Theological Seminary. She and her surgeon husband live in Midwest City, Oklahoma, where they are active in all phases of church life. Though not ordained and not seeking ordination, Lewis regards herself as called to minister and she fulfills that ministry in a multitude of ways in the church and beyond.

The opening paragraph of her address shows a deep commitment to the local church. She said: "I have been in church related positions. However, my real vocation is not church-related, it *is* the church. . . . The church is where we begin and end. We are nurtured and matured to hear a call to prepare to return to minister. Whatever we do in terms of church-relatedness as vocations must be in perspective with the priority scale and value system of the church itself and the will of the Father." [1]

Throughout her paper this influential Baptist woman reflected intense love and loyalty for the church. Though acutely aware of its shortcomings, as well as foot-dragging by the denomination, she took a strong stand as a *church*woman and challenged Southern Baptist women to work out their ministry in relation to the church.

Through the years, no group has been more unfailingly loyal to the church than have Baptist women. They supported missions, taught Sunday School classes, nurtured children in the faith, and generally made themselves indispensible to Baptist progress. Baptist women in the newly emerging forms of ministry insist they have no desire to forsake the church in which they were nurtured and in which they were taught to be open to God's call. They want to minister, and to minister within the boundaries of the church. A few Southern Baptist women have been forced out of the church to find employment in ministry elsewhere, but this has been for the most part against their will. The contemporary movement of Southern Baptist women in ministry is a movement within the church and not outside the church.

One is on more solid ground in describing what has been in the past than in charting what shall be in the future. This book has been primarily historical, setting out the role of Baptist women in the past. However, this last chapter will look at the contemporary situation relating to Baptist women.

Discovery of Women

Women have been around as long as men, and they have ministered in various ways in Baptist churches as long as there have been such churches. However, it appears that Southern Baptists are just now "discovering" women and their potential for ministry. New ideas and attitudes about the role and effectiveness of ministering women surface in various Southern Baptist Convention groups and agencies.

Are Southern Baptist changing their position about women in ministry? This question is difficult to answer. Anything that is alive is changing, and Southern Baptists are no exception. No doubt we are undergoing gradual changes of viewpoint on many subjects, as we have often done in the past. However, the Southern Baptist Convention is structured for cooperative work in missions, evangelism, and Christian education and does not readily lend itself to opinion polling. In short, it is difficult to know what 13,000,000 Southern Baptists think on any subject, or even what their primary leaders think. No doubt they run the gamut of all shades of opinion on the place of women in religion, as they do on other subjects.

However, by selective sampling of opinion of certain Southern Baptist population groups, some have attempted to determine typical

Southern Baptist viewpoints on the present and future roles of women in Baptist churches. As in all polls, there is always a margin of error, and many observers disagree on how large a sampling is necessary to establish valid conclusions. Three such studies are reported here, without any attempt to evaluate their design or validate their conclusions.

In 1977 Clay L. Price of the Home Mission Board conducted a study entitled, "A Survey of Southern Baptist Attitudes Toward the Role of Women in Church and Society." [2] In 1978 he submitted this study to the graduate faculty of West Georgia College in Carrollton, Georgia, as his thesis for a Master of Arts degree. This is probably the most complete and professional survey of Southern Baptist viewpoints on this subject.

Price sent questionnaires to 668 persons, including pastors, WMU directors, Sunday School teachers, and Baptist lay persons—men and women. The return was 389, or 58 percent, considered quite high. The sample was geographically balanced, with 22 percent from the Southeast, 26 percent from the Southwest, 21 percent from the Pioneer East, and 31 percent from the Pioneer West. The survey was also balanced between respondents from small, medium, and large churches.

Only 24 percent of the sample approved the ordination of women to the chaplaincy, and 34 percent approved of women deacons. However, over 75 percent approved of women's being ordained for work in religious education, youth work, or social ministries. Pastors were significantly less open than lay persons to these possibilities.

Perhaps more revealing is the fact that 18 percent of Southern Baptist polled felt the Bible allows the possibility of women serving as pastors. Further, 17 percent would personally approve of women's being pastors, and 16 percent thought women would be effective pastors. Fifteen percent approved of the ordination of women to the pastoral ministry and would be open to the calling of a woman as pastor. However, given the choice between a man and woman as their own pastor, only two persons said they would choose a woman.

Part of the Price survey included the following questions, with this tabulation of responses in percentages. Because not all answered all questions, the percentage totals do not add up to 100.

	Yes	No
1. Would you vote for a woman for President?	34	63
2. Would you vote for a woman for Congress?	68	30
3. Would you vote for a woman for the state legislature?	71	27
4. Can women run businesses as well as men?	67	29
5. Can women fulfill pastoral roles effectively?	16	80
6. Can women understand politics as well as men?	73	23
7. Do you approve of women entering business and professional positions traditionally open only to men?	62	35
8. Do you approve of women serving as ministers?	17	80
9. Do women have as good a chance as men to be an executive?	30	65
10. All in all, do you favor or oppose most of the efforts to strengthen and change women's status in society?	41 Favor	55 Oppose
11. According to your understanding of the Bible, does the possibility exist for women to serve in pastoral roles?	18	78
12. If an equally qualified man and woman were available for the pastorate of a given Baptist church, which would you honestly choose?	95 Man	— Woman

	Yes	No
13. Do you approve the ordination of women to the pastoral ministry?	15	82
14. Do you approve the ordination of women to specific areas of service, such as:		
Chaplaincy	24	71
Religious Education	76	21
Youth Work	78	19
Social Ministries (Weekday, Daycare)	80	17
15. If a qualified woman were available for the pastorate of a given Baptist church, would you be open to calling her?	15	81
16. Do you approve women serving as deaconesses?	34	63
17. Do you think attitudes toward women in the ministry will change significantly within the next 25 years?	66	30

According to this survey, most Southern Baptist are quite supportive of women's advances in society, and also in nonpastoral roles in the church. Education seems to have a greater effect on attitudes than either age or region, with those having more than high school education significantly more open to leadership roles for women in church and society. Significantly, two-thirds of the respondents expect Southern Baptists to move toward greater acceptance of women in ministry in the next twenty-five years.

If this survey reflects a fair sampling of Southern Baptists, then possibly attitudes toward men in ministry have already changed significantly in the past generation. Price concluded that "as the roles of women expand in society, Southern Baptist churches will have to consider to a greater degree the involvement of women in the church." [3]

In early 1978 Charles V. Petty conducted a survey of practices relating to women in Baptist churches in North Carolina. Petty, at that time executive director of the Christian Life Council of the Baptist State Convention of North Carolina, sent the following questionnaire to 80 Directors of Missions in the state.

ROLE OF WOMEN IN NORTH CAROLINA BAPTIST LIFE IN THE _____ ASSOCIATION

1. Has your association taken a stand for or against leadership roles of women?

   ____For   ____Against   ____Has taken no stand

2. Have any churches in your association ordained women as deacons?

   ____Yes   ____No

   If yes, approximately how many have done so?

   ____churches

3. Have any churches in your association ordained women to the ministry?

   ____Yes   ____No   ____Don't know

   If yes, approximately how many have done so?

   ____churches

4. Do any Baptist churches in your association have women deacons still living from the time before World War I when many Baptist churches had women deacons?

   ____Yes   ____No   ____Don't know

5. Are you aware of any change in the attitudes of Southern Baptists in North Carolina for or against the leadership role of women in Baptist life?

   ____Yes   ____No   ____Don't know

   If yes, is the change predominantly for or against? (circle one)

Reports were returned from 66 of the associations. Since not all answered all questions, the totals do not add up to the total number of respondents.

According to these reports, 57 associations had taken no stand on the role of women in church, though two associations had voted in favor of leadership roles for women and one had voted against such roles. Forty directors reported that churches in their associations had ordained women deacons, with a total of 128 churches known to have done so. Only three associations reported churches with women deacons (or deaconesses) still living from the World War I era, when such a practice was fairly common.

Twelve directors reported that churches in their associations had ordained women to the ministry, with a total of 18 such ordinations reported. A number of others had been licensed, presumably looking toward ordination later. Thirty-eight directors reported that churches in their areas were undergoing changes of attitude toward women in ministry, of which 36 reported the changes were toward more acceptance of women in ministry. Ten reported no change, 13 had no opinion, and one reported a shift toward more opposition to women.

One director reported that churches in his area favored change "when it is taking place somewhere else," and opposed change "when it is a threat at home." The same respondent wrote that: "Some women and young men (and young pastors) are crusaders for "women's liberation." The people generally have adjusted to the idea that it is inevitable and are resigned to it whether they like it or not. Several churches have ordained women deacons. Some of these did so because they did not have qualified men, and some did so as a concession to insistant [sic] female voices in the church." [4]

Interestingly, several of these directors of missions are themselves women. Though some of them serve in the more conservative associations, without exception the women reported changes in their areas favoring more leadership roles for women. One association reported the likelihood of a woman as moderator, and several reported they had made diligent efforts to include qualified women among associational officers.

While not pretending to be a scientific polling because of the restricted sampling, these reports from Directors of Missions about trends in churches in their areas are quite revealing. Perhaps the most significant aspect is not what is presently happening there, but the overwhelming agreement that further changes are coming, and that these will be in the direction of more freedom and openness toward women in ministry.

Another survey, even more restricted, was conducted by Minette

Drumwright at the Glorieta and Ridgecrest Baptist Conference centers in the summer of 1977. Mrs. Drumwright a popular speaker and writer on the role of Baptist churchwomen, is well-known for her work in Woman's Missionary Union. She wrote *Women in the Church,* a study guide and lesson plans for a study of women in the Bible, in history, and in present church work. In preparing for writing this material, Drumwright drew up a questionnaire designed to gauge women's current attitudes toward their own roles in the home and church. During WMU weeks at both Glorieta and Ridgecrest, the survey was filled out by approximately 3,000 Baptist women of all ages.

The Drumwright questionnaire presented a series of statements, and respondents were asked to register agreement or disagreement. The exact form of the statements differed slightly between Glorieta and Ridgecrest, but since the variety was very slight, only the Ridgecrest form is reported here. The accompanying chart shows some of the statements and responses.

No one, including Mrs. Drumwright, would claim this as a scientific sampling of Southern Baptist viewpoints about women in the church. Since this was a WMU conference, the respondents were all women. Also one notes that those who attend denominational conferences at the summer assemblies may not represent a typical sampling of lay people in the churches. Even so, this is a most revealing survey in that it shows great interest and openness toward Baptist women in ministry.

Most respondents in this survey agreed that Jesus violated customs of his day in his open attitude toward women, and about half agreed that Paul's restrictive statements about women applied only to local situations in the Bible. A significant percentage of respondents believe that the New Testament churches had women deacons, and that women in Baptist churches today should be eligible for election as deacons. Somewhat fewer believe that women should be ordained as ministers, though more than 50 percent in some age groups agreed that God may call women as well as men to ministry.

Some regional and age differences showed up in this survey, with older women being significantly more open to the possibility of women in ministry than was true of younger women. Respondents at Ridgecrest also registered more acceptance of women in ministry than did those surveyed at Glorieta.

These surveys, incomplete as they are, show that significant numbers of Southern Baptists are open to the idea of women's serving as deacons and ministers. They also reveal that Baptist interpretation of Bible passages, at least for some, no longer forbids women to be active in church roles.

A New Awareness

It was small, as Southern Baptist meetings go, but its potential impact was far-reaching. For three days in September, 1978, about 235 women and 60 men gathered in Nashville for the first Consultation on Women in Church-Related Vocations. Limited by invitation to 300 participants, this consultation was sponsored by eleven agencies of the Southern Baptist Convention.

One session featured the heads of SBC agencies in a question and answer period. One woman raised a question about whether the agency heads had really tried to employ women and given them equal opportunity for advancement. Pressing her question, she repeated, "Have you, have you?" The agency leader chosen to respond for the group admitted, "No, I have not, not really. But in the future I shall be more aware of this issue and more sensitive, because you have caused me to face the question."

"More aware and more sensitive." That may be the major result of the entire Consultation. Certainly the participants, including a group of very low-profile men, left the meeting more aware and more sensitive.

The consultation grew, indirectly, out of the Bold Mission Thrust program of the Southern Baptist Convention. In an Interagency Council discussion of how to enlist Southern Baptist participation in that program, a question arose about the motivation and enlistment of women in convention causes. The two women on the Interagency Council suggested the need for a more thoroughgoing discussion of the involvement of Southern Baptist women, and this led eventually to plans for the consultation. It was officially sponsored by the Baptist Joint Committee, Brotherhood Commission, Christian Life Commission, Foreign Mission Board, Radio and Television Commission,

"WOMEN IN THE CHURCH" QUESTIONNAIRE

	Age Group Location	18-30 G	18-30 R	31-45 G	31-45 R	46-60 G	46-60 R	Over 60 G	Over 60 R
1. God's intention for man/woman relationships is partnership rather than one's being subordinate to the other.	Agree	86%	79%	94%	86%	97%	91%	98%	95%
	Disagree	13%	20%	6%	12%	2%	8%	–	4.5%
	Uncertain	1%	1%	–	2%	1%	1%	2%	.5%
2. God intends for only men to have places of leadership in situations that include both men and women.	Agree	20%	9%	11%	9%	9%	5%	7%	10%
	Disagree	79%	87%	85%	89%	84%	92%	88%	87%
	Uncertain	1%	4%	4%	2%	7%	2%	5%	3%
3. Men have more responsibility before God than women do.	Agree	21%	18%	17%	14%	17%	8%	12%	9%
	Disagree	76%	77%	80%	84%	80%	90%	85%	90%
	Uncertain	3%	5%	3%	2%	3%	2%	3%	1%
4. Women should always yield to a man's decision.	Agree	13%	10%	10%	8%	4%	4%	3%	3%
	Disagree	74%	84%	80%	89%	93%	93%	92%	94%
	Uncertain	13%	6%	10%	3%	3%	3%	5%	3%
5. Jesus related to women in a way that violated the custom of the day.	Agree	68%	80%	78%	82%	77%	80%	68%	72%
	Disagree	16%	12%	15%	13%	19%	17%	27%	23%
	Uncertain	16%	8%	7%	4%	4%	3%	5%	5%

6. Some of Paul's teachings apply to the local situations to which he was writing and are not intended to be applied to all churches for all time.	Agree	43%	43%	54%	51%	50%	54%	52%	50%
	Disagree	42%	41%	37%	43%	43%	25%	40%	40%
	Uncertain	15%	16%	9%	6%	7%	21%	8%	10%
7. Some of the New Testament churches had women deacons.	Agree	31%	45%	32%	49%	25%	53%	33%	52%
	Disagree	42%	32%	44%	25%	54%	28%	40%	31%
	Uncertain	27%	28%	24%	26%	21%	19%	27%	17%
8. Qualified women should be eligible for election as deacons in my church.	Agree	29%	36%	20%	45%	23%	49%	24%	49%
	Disagree	55%	50%	67%	40%	77%	38%	57%	38%
	Uncertain	16%	14%	13%	15%	—	13%	18%	13%
9. Women should be ordained to the ministry if they feel God has called them.	Agree	22%	52%	18%	51%	12%	49%	10%	52%
	Disagree	61%	28%	69%	31%	73%	30%	71%	27%
	Uncertain	17%	20%	13%	18%	15%	21%	19%	21%
10. God calls only men to the pastoral ministry.	Agree	39%	27%	44%	28%	49%	30%	46%	25%
	Disagree	37%	50%	33%	49%	28%	50%	26%	55%
	Uncertain	24%	23%	23%	23%	24%	20%	28%	20%
11. God intends that women should be subordinate to men in the home.	Agree	47%	39%	35%	37%	16%	30%	13%	31%
	Disagree	50%	52%	62%	57%	81%	64%	84%	64%
	Uncertain	3%	9%	3%	6%	2%	6%	3%	5%
12. God intends that women should be subordinate to men in the church.	Agree	32%	29%	24%	22%	13%	16%	11%	18%
	Disagree	56%	57%	68%	67%	84%	74%	83%	73%
	Uncertain	12%	14%	8%	11%	3%	10%	6%	8%

Southeastern Baptist Theological Seminary, Southern Baptist Theological Seminary, Sunday School Board, and Women's Missionary Union.

The consultation was designed "to develop a body of findings for use by all denominational agencies in employment, policymaking, education programs, and vocational guidance" for Southern Baptists. Toward that outcome, the consultation began with three stated objectives: (1) to define the present situation in the SBC with regard to women in church-related vocations; (2) to provide a platform for the presentation of a balanced variety of views on the topic; and (3) to identify and explain the options now available for women and girls now considering church-related vocations.

With a steering committee chaired by Catherine Allen of Woman's Missionary Union, the consultation included major addresses, Bible study sessions, and small group discussions. Though many women present were ordained ministers and deacons, the consultation never became a forum to debate the ordination issue. "Southern Baptist women aspire to thousands of jobs which have no relation to ordination," said one speaker. The primary focus was church-related vocations, and ordination was dealt with primarily as it arose as a requirement for some church employment.

No doubt the women encouraged and strengthened each other as they shared testimonies about their sense of call and commitment to ministry. Some shared their fulfillment in ministry without ordination; others told of call, education, and ordination, with still no place in which to minister. Several young women seminarians attended the consultation and gave uniform voice to a plea for changes in seminary faculties and curricula. They expressed a desire for more female models in ministry, including more women faculty, chapel speakers, campus chaplains, and supply preachers.

Kay Shurden of Louisville, Kentucky, presented a highly acclaimed research paper in which she sought to demonstrate that SBC Sunday School Board publications generally present and reinforce stereotyped roles for girls and women in subordination to males. Perhaps most of the women present would have agreed with Elaine Dickson, church services and materials coordinator for the Sunday School Board, who said the real issue for Baptist women is not identity—knowing who they are—but finding a place to function and serve.

At this writing, the book of findings from this consultation is not yet available. However, from the response of those who attended and from preliminary reports in various Baptist papers, one senses that this will prove to be a most significant meeting. As a result, Baptist women will probably be more united, more informed, and perhaps more uninhibited in speaking out about their sense of call to ministry. No doubt the men will also be more informed, more aware, and more sensitive to the religious aspirations and abilities of the other half of the race. One could well agree with Len Sehested of Fort Worth, who said of the consultation, "Perhaps the most important thing is that we are *here*. And we will be heard."

Women in Waiting

One of the most disconcerting aspects of the consultation was the testimony of many young women who have graduated from seminary, and still cannot find a suitable place of service in Baptist life. In some form this testimony was heard repeatedly, "I have a call, a degree, plenty of recommendations, and some experience—but no job."

Some Baptist women struggle with unemployment, underemployment, and unsuitable employment. Of course, these problems are not limited to women. Some men also find, to their despair, that a seminary degree does not guarantee a call as pastor of a church. However, the problem is much more acute with women, who often have to settle either for secular employment of church employment far below their goal and training.

This raises a serious question for Southern Baptists. Enrollments in the six SBC seminaries are mushrooming, with about 15 percent of that enrollment being women. In the school year 1977-78 there were over 1,600 women enrolled in Southern Baptist seminaries. Some of them were preparing for the usual "women's jobs" in the church, like church secretary and children's workers. However, many of them, and a rapidly increasing group, were preparing for some form of ministry, including the pastorate.

In order for these women to enroll in seminary, they must have a letter of recommendation from their home churches. Many Baptist women, and some men, are asking about the dilemma of a church that will recommend a young woman for admission to seminary, but will not consider her for a church position upon graduation. Many are urging more honest counseling of girls and young women considering ministry so they will see a more accurate picture of the obstacles they will face upon graduation.

Who are these young women, and why are they in seminary? They are our own daughters and sisters, who have grown up in our churches where they heard the gospel and responded to the claims of Christ. They have listened to countless sermons on the need for workers in God's Kingdom, the call of God, and the fields that are white unto harvest. They not only have heard those sermons; they have heeded them and taken them seriously. With every evidence of sincerity and moral earnestness they say God has called *them* to service, and they seek ways to follow that call.

With multitudes of women in our churches, colleges, and seminaries who profess a sense of call and who have undeniable gifts, the issue of Southern Baptist women in ministry assumes a new perspective. It is no longer merely a dull debate over historical precedents or a theoretical discussion of ancient texts, but a pressing practical problem. Has God called these women? If he has, dare we impede their efforts to serve? Surrounded by pressing needs, how can we refuse the aid of people who appear capable and qualified? It may well be that these practical concerns will outweigh more theoretical arguments in shaping the ultimate decisions of Southern Baptists about the role of women.

Conclusion

This book has been an effort to trace the changing roles of women in Baptist life, from our earliest history to the present. The evidence suggests clearly that those roles have changed and are rapidly changing today.

A century ago a Southern Baptist pastor observed, "The sisterhood of our Southern Zion is rising." Apparently that is even more true in our generation.

Notes

[1] Unpublished paper, September, 1978.
[2] Clay L. Price, "A Survey of Southern Baptist Attitudes Toward the

Role of Women in Church and Society," (Unpublished M.A. Thesis, West Georgia College, Carrollton, Georgia, 1978).

[3] Ibid., 101.

[4] Charles V. Petty, Survey on the Role of Women in North Carolina Baptist Life, 1978, unpublished.

For Further Reading

Books

ANDERS, SARAH FRANCES. *Woman Alone: Confident and Creative.* Tennessee: Broadman Press, 1976.

BEAVER, R. PIERCE. *All Loves Excelling: American Protestant Women in World Missions.* Grand Rapids: William B. Eerdmans, 1968.

BLISS, KATHLEEN. *The Service and Status of Women in the Churches.* London: SCM Press, Ltd., 1952.

BOCKELMAN, WILFRED. *Gothard, the Man and His Ministry.* Michigan: Quill Publication, 1976.

BOLDREY, RICHARD and JOYCE. *Chauvinist or Feminist: Paul's View of Women.* Grand Rapids: Baker Book House, 1976.

BROADUS, JOHN A. *Should Women Speak in Mixed Public Assemblies?* Louisville: Baptist Book Concern, Inc., 1904.

CALKINS, GLADYS GILKEY. *Follow These Women: A History of the Development of United Work Among Women of the Protestant Churches in the United States.* New York: National Council of Churches, 1961.

COX, ETHLENE BOONE. *Following in His Train.* Nashville: Broadman Press, 1938.

DALY, MARY. *The Church and the Second Sex.* New York: Harper & Row, 1968.

ERMARTH, MARGARET SITTLER. *Adam's Fractured Rib.* Philadelphia: Fortress Press, 1970.

GIBSON, ELSIE. *When the Minister is a Woman.* New York: Holt, Rinehart & Winston, 1970.

HANAFORD, PHOEBE A. *Daughters of America.* Augusta, Maine: True and Company, 1882.

HARKNESS, GEORGIA. *Women in Church and Society.* New York: Abingdon Press, 1972.

HOLLIS, HARRY N., JR., Comp. *Christian Freedom for Women and*

Other Human Beings. Nashville: Broadman Press, 1974.

LETSINGER, NORMAN HERBERT. *The Women's Liberation Movement: Implications for Southern Baptists.* Louisville: Southern Baptist Theological Seminary, Th.D. Dissertation, 1973.

LOLLIS, LORRAINE. *The Shape of Adam's Rib: A Lively History of Women's Work in the Christian Church.* St. Louis: The Bethany Press, 1970.

MEYER, RUTH FRITZ. *Women on a Mission: The Role of Women in the Church from Bible Times up to and Including a History of Lutheran Women's Missionary League.* St. Louis: Concordia Publishing House, 1967.

MONTGOMERY, HELEN BARRETT. *Western Home in Eastern Lands.* New York: Macmillan, 1911.

PAPACHRISOU, JUDITH. *Women Together.* New York: Alfred A. Knopf, 1976.

PROCTOR, PRISCILLA and WILLIAM. *Women in the Pulpit.* Garden City, New York: Doubleday and Company, 1976.

PROHL, RUSSELL C. *Woman in the Church.* Grand Rapids: Wm. B. Eerdmans Publishing Co., 1957.

RUETHER, ROSEMARY RADFORD, ed. *Religion and Sexism: Images of Woman in the Jewish and Christian Traditions.* New York: Simon and Shuster, 1974.

RYRIE, CHARLES R. *The Place of Women in the Church.* New York: Macmillan Company, 1958.

SCANZONI, LETHA and HARDESTY, NANCY. *All We're Meant to Be: A Biblical Approach to Women's Liberation.* Waco: Word Books, 1974.

STENDAHL, KRISTER. *The Bible and the Role of Women.* Philadelphia: Fortress Press, 1966.

VAIL, ALBERT L. *Mary Webb and the Mother Society.* Philadelphia: American Baptist Publication Society, 1914.

VERDESI, ELIZABETH HOWELL. *In But Still Out: Women in the Church.* Philadelphia: The Westminster Press, 1973.

WILLIAMS, DON. *The Apostle Paul and Women in the Church.* Van Nuys, California: BIM Publishing Company, 1977.

Articles

ANDERS, SARAH FRANCES. "The Role of Women in American Religion." *Southwestern Journal of Theology,* Spring, 1976.

———— "The State of the Second Sex: Emancipation or Explosion? *The Baptist Student,* May, 1974.

CATE, ROBERT L. "Shall We Have Women Deacons?" *Baptist Standard,* April 17, 1974.

DEWEESE, CHARLES W. "Deaconesses in Baptist Work in the Northwest." *Baptist History and Heritage,* January, 1977.

ELLIOT, ELIZABETH. "Why I Oppose the Ordination of Women." *Christianity Today,* June 6, 1975.

FALLS, HELEN EMERY. "Baptist Women in Missions Support in the Nineteenth Century." *Baptist History and Heritage,* January, 1977.

FILIPI, EMILY. "What's Happening of the Women?" *The Quarterly Review,* April-May-June, 1970.

HAWTHORNE, MELVIN. "Deaconesses Ordained in Manhattan Baptist Church." *Church Administration,* August, 1971.

HINSON, E. GLENN. "The Church: Liberator or Oppressor of Women?" *Review and Expositor,* Winter, 1975.

———— "On The Election of Women as Deacons." *The Deacon,* April, 1973.

JEWETT, PAUL. "Why I Favor the Ordination of Women." *Christianity Today,* June 6, 1975.

JONES, MARY NEAL. "Ordination Not Only Role for Women in Ministry." *Illinois Baptist,* March 30, 1977.

LETSINGER, NORMAN H. "The Status of Women in the Southern Baptist Convention in Historical Perspective." *Baptist History and Heritage,* January, 1977.

LOCKETT, DARBY RICHARDSON. "Feminist Footholds in Religion." *Foundations,* January-March, 1976.

LUMPKIN, WILLIAM L. "The Role of Women in the 18th Century Virginia Baptist Life." *Baptist History and Heritage,* July, 1973.

MANN, GERALD E. "How We Got Women Deacons." *The Deacon,* April, 1975.

PASCHALL, G. W. "Morgan Edwards' Materials Towards a History of the Baptist in the Province of North Carolina (1772)." *The North Carolina Historical Review,* VII, July, 1930.

SUMNERS, BILL. "Southern Baptists and Women's Right to Vote, 1910-1920." *Baptist History and Heritage,* January, 1977.